PARENT

A Guide for R_____ _____ _____en in Today's World

IRIS YANKELEVICH

Psychologist / Psychotherapist

Forest Hills, NY

November 6, 2013

DEDICATION

I dedicate this book to my two children, Ariela and Juan Noé, and my grandchildren, Gaby, Laura, Anabel and Simone. You give me the motivation to write and the inspiration to live. I love you unconditionally.

CONTENTS

ACKNOWLEDGMENTS

First of all, I'd like to thank Slava Osowska, my translator and editor. Thank you for your collaboration and all of your helpful comments. I'd also like to thank Dr. Randolph Ortiz for all the input and support he gave me during this process. Thank you to Amin Torres, who designed the cover. And finally, I am grateful to all the parents who have participated in my seminars and workshops. Thank you for sharing your questions and concerns. You have contributed immensely to this book.

PROLOGUE

I've always thought that childrearing is like holding a wet bar of soap—you can't squeeze too much or hold on too loosely. You can't hold the soap sideways. The pressure and balance have to be just right to keep it from slipping.

> How do you love children without smothering them?

> How do you protect them without stunting their growth?

> How do you guide them without doing everything for them?

> How do you give them freedom without neglecting them?

> How do you keep them out of danger without coddling them?

To do these things, you need a lot of common sense, intuition, and maturity, but above all, you need knowledge, which is why it's so important for parents today to keep themselves informed—to read, attend conferences and seminars, and join study groups.

In the past, generational changes weren't as big as they are today. Parents passed down to their children the things they had been taught, and their children passed those same things down to their children—how to educate, protect, and give guidance. Nowadays, though, if you just do exactly what your parents did, it's not going to work—the world is changing enormously. Our children are growing up in a world that is very different from the one that we grew up in.

Mankind is always evolving. Just a few generations ago, babies didn't open their eyes until fifteen days after they were born, and they couldn't support their own heads until they were two months old. Now children are born with their eyes open and they hold their head up within a few short weeks. And then there's television, the internet, and the fact that nowadays, children are allowed to participate in our conversations. Children develop faster. They reason, demand, correct, judge, and even compete with their parents. When we were growing up, that was unheard of.

The issue is not whether this is better or worse. It is what it is. It's like sailing a boat. It's not about changing the course of the wind, but setting the sails to our advantage. If we turn the sails into the wind that was blowing yesterday, our boat isn't going to move where we want it to today.

Seeking information isn't a sign of weakness or ignorance. On the contrary, it is a sign of wisdom and strength. Learning to be a parent in today's world is not an easy task, but it's not impossible if you get the information and guidance that you need. Notice I say *learning* to be parents. We used to learn how to be parents from our parents. And it's not that they were wrong, but it just won't work anymore. We need other sources.

This book is my humble contribution to this learning process. My goal is to get you to think about the effects of everything you do or say to your children, to think about what you want to achieve, and let that be your motivation, rather than your impulses or fears—because the best way to make your fears a reality is to be afraid.

Parents with children of all ages are having enormous difficulty, and they are finding little guidance. It used to be enough to get advice from your grandparents or other family members, or to seek religious counsel, but that's no longer enough. Our reality has changed, and we have a whole new set of problems to address.

GETTING CHILDREN TO RESPECT LIMITS

Setting limits for children is one of the most difficult tasks that parents face, especially since our society's sense of authority has changed. We can no longer just say, "You need to obey me. I'm your father (or mother)!" Your child will probably ask, "Why *should* I?" A generation ago, no child would have even thought about asking that question, but nowadays, children question, talk back, complain, and react instinctively to any limitations placed on them.

Bedtime has turned into a nightmare for Nicole, whose daughter, Emma, is five-years old. Despite the fact that the little girl is exhausted from shopping all afternoon, Emma doesn't want to go to bed. "It's the same struggle every night," says Nicole. "She doesn't want to be alone. She asks me to stay with her, to bring her a glass of water, 'don't turn the lights off,' 'sleep with me.' I feel cruel for leaving her alone in her room. I always want my little girl to be happy and I can't bear it when she cries and asks me to do something that I know I can do."

The problem isn't just that Nicole wants her daughter to

obey a bedtime rule—she also wants the little girl to be happy about the limit she is setting. We all react negatively to limits at first, but we eventually do get used to them. From an early age, our instinct is to rebel against limits. No one is happy about being unable to park the car where we want to, but then we realize that it's just the way things are. It isn't worth it to complain or rebel. And the same is true of children. At first they'll react against a "no," but if that "no" is a firm one, they'll come to accept it.

Wanting her daughter to accept and be happy about a limit, Nicole fell into a trap. We need to be able to accept the fact that when we say "no," our child may not like it, and they might even try to pressure us by crying or screaming, with pained expressions and manipulative phrases like, "I don't love you anymore." And that's when we fall into the trap.

If we don't stay firm, it will become impossible to set any limits, and we'll end up letting the child do whatever they want. When children feel that any attempt by their parents to set limits will end in failure, they feel emboldened and powerful, and they begin to think that the world revolves around them. If it isn't done from the outset, it will become harder and harder to set limits as the child grows up, and by the time they become a teenager, it will be practically impossible. Some parents begin to feel like their child has them in the palm of their hand.

Parents who are divorced often find they can't be firm with their children as a result of their feelings of guilt. Some mothers feel guilty for not having been able to keep the father at home, or for not having chosen a better father in the first place, and fathers who leave often feel guilty for abandoning the home or for not spending as much time with their children as they would have liked. Children take advantage of those feelings. From early on, they learn to observe their parents' weaknesses and use them to their advantage. But we can't let ourselves be taken in by the "sad little eyes" that our children sometimes show us when we don't let them do what they want.

Set a Rule, Define it Clearly

Let's say we don't want our children to eat too much candy, but we leave a box of sweets on the table and tell them not to eat a lot of them. The child's response will be, "But, Mom, I didn't have a lot." (Of course not, it was only half the package).

Children don't understand quantity. They don't know what "a lot" means. Mother may think something is too much, but for them, it's not enough. Instead, take three or four sweets out of the box, hand them to the child and say, "You can have three today, and tomorrow I'll give you three more."

If your child goes out bike riding, and you say, "Don't go too far!" when they come home, your child might say, "I didn't! It was just over there!" (And maybe "over there" means 50 blocks away). What's far for Mother is close for the child. Instead, say, "Don't go past the supermarket two blocks down," or "Don't go beyond the gas station on Vermont Street."

If you tell a teenager, "Don't come back late!" and they show up at two in the morning, when you ask them about it, they'll probably say, "Two in the morning is not late!" What we really need to say is, "Be home before midnight." It is important for rules to be well-defined and clear. We should never use ambiguous words like "a lot," "a little," "far" or "late." These words are abstract, and everyone—especially children—will find convenient ways to interpret them.

Don't make rules that you aren't willing to follow.

We often tell our children that it is not good to lie, and yet when the telephone rings, we tell our child, "If it's for me, tell them I'm not here." Children learn mostly by example, not by words.

Six-year-old Logan said to his father, "You told me I shouldn't hit kids who are younger than me, so how come you're allowed to hit me?" Children understand that rules are for everyone and what's wrong for one person is wrong for everyone. What good is it for parents to tell their child not to smoke, if they're smokers? Will their child respect them?

The mother of a nine-year-old girl comes to my office worried that her daughter is overweight. "Jasmine is always going to the refrigerator. She eats a lot of bread and sweets like ice cream and candy," her mother says. When I explain that her child needs to get on a low-sugar, low-carbohydrate diet, she says, "If my husband comes home and he doesn't find any cake, or cookies or bread, he goes nuts. He'll buy that stuff himself and bring it home anyway."

"Is your husband overweight, too?" I ask.

"Well yes," says Jasmine's mother. "He weighs 240 pounds and is only five foot six…. He could stand to lose 70 pounds."

If this family isn't willing to change the way they eat and keep the sweets and the flour to a minimum, how can they ask their child to? Children develop willpower by observing it in their parents, and they develop honesty and truthfulness by watching. Parents can only make demands when they practice what they preach.

Be consistent. Don't change the rules every day.

If we want a child to turn off the TV and go to bed every night at nine o'clock, we have to make sure they follow this rule every day. Let's say we set a bedtime rule, and then one day when we have company over, it's more convenient for us to let the child keep watching TV past their bedtime so that they don't start becoming a nuisance. The next day when we tell the child to turn the TV off and go to bed, they're bound to say, "But last night you let me stay up until eleven. Why do I have to go to bed at nine tonight?"

When children see that rules can be broken easily, or that they can be broken when it is convenient, then they want to be able to bend the rules too. Children see Mom and Dad changing the rules when it's convenient for them, and they can't understand why they can't do the same thing. If you're going to adjust their bedtime or their dinnertime, or change any other rule, tell your child beforehand, and give them a valid reason for the change: "For now, you'll turn off the TV at eight o'clock and go to bed. When you're on summer vacation, you can go to bed an hour or two later."

We need to be careful not to give in too often and to make sure that the child isn't manipulating us. If children discover that by crying or by making a nuisance of themselves, they can get what they want, they'll do it every day. If they find out that they can get Mother to give in and buy them something by screaming and yelling inside a store, they'll do it every time. In such cases, we need to be firm, and make them understand that they can cry and kick and scream all they want, but they won't get everything they ask for. Instead, they'll be taken right back home without getting anything at all. A child may repeat the scene two or three times to test just how firm Mother really is, but later, they will learn that Mother only buys them something when she can, and when *she* wants to.

Be Balanced

Clearly, we don't want to turn our homes into a military regiment. We need to know when to be flexible and when to be firm. When our child doesn't comply with a certain order, we should listen to their reasoning, and when it's valid, accept it. We can take special occasions like the child's birthday into account, and say, "Today is special. You can go to bed later, but starting tomorrow, we go back to our usual bedtime."

The word "discipline" comes from the Latin *disciplina,* which means teaching or learning. Therefore, to discipline a child means to teach them, to show them right from wrong. It doesn't mean punishment, which is how many parents interpret the word. Punishment doesn't teach. On the contrary, it leads to rebelliousness. When we want to teach our children something, we should explain ourselves and give guidance. If the child doesn't accept what we say, make them feel the consequences—not through punishment, but through the effects of their actions.

HOW TO CHANGE INAPPROPRIATE BEHAVIOR

Finding non-destructive ways to change behaviors in children can be a major challenge for parents. The first step is to prioritize which behaviors we want to change. What are the most aggressive behaviors, or the ones that bother other parents, teachers and siblings the most? These types of behaviors create problems in relationships and affect children's self-esteem.

Look at the following list and mark the inappropriate behaviors that you would like your children to stop, and if your son or daughter has a behavior issue that isn't listed, add it.

- Hitting adults or other children
- Screaming and crying when they don't get their way
- Making fun of other children or adults
- Aggressively throwing things
- Talking back or yelling when told what to do
- Yanking toys away from other children

- Intentionally breaking household items or toys
- Kicking other people
- Biting others
- Pulling others' hair
- Spitting at other people
- Persistently interrupting when others are talking
- Mistreating or injuring animals
- Damaging clothing or furniture
- Picking fights or intentionally looking for trouble
- Being bossy and demanding
- Constantly whining
- Disobeying adults
- Foul language
- Making offensive faces or gestures at others
- Demanding that their parents buy them something every time they go out together
- Crying and throwing tantrums to get what they want
- Lying or covering up something that they've done
- Refusing to help when asked
- Making rude noises

Here we should only be considering frequent behavior. If it's something that only happens every once in a while, then try to figure out why your child acted the way they did, and make it clear that it is not to happen again.

Ignoring Inappropriate Behavior

A simple technique to change unwanted, isolated behavior is to just ignore it, not to dignify it with attention. Clearly, this can only work if the behavior has not fully "taken root" and become habitual. Getting attention is often at the root of these behaviors, and it plays a very important role in their repetition. Attention from their parents is extremely important to children, and it could be that some of their actions are focused on getting it.

Many children discover that "being bad" gets them the most attention, and that's why they do those things over and over, until they become habits. Many parents say, "I give my child a lot of attention when they do good things, too." But if you give the same amount of attention to good and bad things, you won't "alter the balance" between these two kinds of behavior. That's why it is important to give their positive actions plenty of attention, while ignoring the negative ones as much as possible. For example, if children talk back, ignore it in that moment, but let them know that it makes you happy when they act respectful. That way, the child will feel that they get more attention for being good than when they behave badly. Sometimes, there might only be a slight improvement in the way the child responds to you. Even if their behavior still hasn't gotten quite right, let your child know that you've taken note, and express satisfaction with how much progress has been made already.

Remember, every child needs attention and appreciation. It's like when you get to the office after getting a haircut, and everybody compliments you. You'll probably continue wearing your hair that way—because we all need approval from others. We need to see a positive image of ourselves reflected in the eyes of other people. It's what motivates us.

When talking to children, it's important to use affectionate words and phrases as well as physical displays of affection like hugs and caresses—but not "material gifts." Ignoring behavior that you don't like isn't easy, so be prepared for what will happen when you do it. To get your attention, they'll yell even louder and be even more insistent, but once you've chosen the specific behavior that you plan to ignore, say to yourself, "I'm aware that to get my attention, Michael or Heather will kick and scream and start crying. Paying attention to that will only reinforce their behavior, and they'll figure out exactly what they need to do for me to react." Continue talking to yourself in a positive way to help you stand firm. Eventually your child will realize that there's nothing to be gained from their behavior. They'll calm down, get worn out, fall asleep, or simply start playing.

Changing Behavior with the "Time-Out"

Because of the excellent results it renders in changing bad behavior, the "Time-Out" is a widely used technique that many books have been written about. This technique consists of removing the child from any stimulus or activity for a short period of time. For example, if a little boy hits his sister when he's been told not to, he should be told to go to his room (**if they feel bored there**), or to the bathroom, or to some other room in the house, along with an alarm clock set to go off at a certain time. A general rule of thumb is one minute for each year of the child's age. In other words, if the child is five years old, the time-out—in which the child is forced to sit still in the designated room—should be five minutes long. It is important to use no more than ten words to tell the child to take a time-out, and also this should be done in less than ten seconds. The time-out needs to be an immediate consequence for their bad behavior. For the duration of the time-out, no one should have contact of any kind with the child, or play with them. And, of course, the child should not be allowed to watch television or listen to the radio. The child should not be holding any toys or have them anywhere nearby. When the timer (kitchen timers work well) or the alarm clock goes off, the child should be told they can go back to their normal activities. But first they should be asked if they know why they were sent to time-out. They should answer this question out loud. It's a way of making them aware of what they've done and that it's an immediate consequence for their behavior. This technique is especially recommended for dealing with children who act aggressive or impulsive.

That said, you should not abuse the time-out technique by using it too often or for too many reasons. Determine a particular behavior you wish to change, and use the time-out every time your child does it.

Some "Time-Out" Rules

The location of the time-out should be a place where the child can be alone and will not be distracted by any outside stimuli. Never place the child under lock and key, however, and never place them in a place that is dark or without sufficient ventilation.

The presence of a clock is important—an external, inanimate object that just keeps track of time. Make sure Mom or Dad is not the one standing watch.

During the time-out, many parents make the mistake of reading to their child or turning on the radio. That makes the technique ineffective. The whole idea is for the child to feel bored, so they won't want to do it again.

THE TRUE MEANING OF CHILD'S PLAY

Many parents think that children are "wasting time" when they play. David, who has a six-year-old son, says, "As soon as Nicholas gets home from school, he does his homework. Then his mother takes him to the library. On Tuesdays and Thursdays, he goes to karate class. The rest of the time, I take him to work with me so he can help out. I want him to learn to be responsible from the outset."

"When does he play?" we ask.

"Oh, I don't allow that," he says. "I don't want my son wasting time on such silliness."

While it is important for children to do their homework regularly, go to the library, practice sports, and help their parents out, it is also vital that they have time to play.

Children channel their frustrations during play. They develop their dreams and fantasies. They confront conflicts and they learn to resolve them. And they have new experiences. "Exploration" also benefits their language and learning abilities.

At about age two, a child can already turn a cardboard

box into a bus or two chairs into a train. Using just their imagination, and a small number of items, they can build a world that isn't there. Later, this ability to give different uses to a single object leads to their comprehension of numbers, letters and abstract ideas. This is where thinking actually begins.

"Go to bed right now!" Nathan orders his teddy bear. "It's time to go to sleep!" "Mommy, you be my cousin Isabella and I'll be the teacher," Emily suggests to her mother. This type of game is called "symbolic play." It's when a broomstick turns into a pony or when a chair becomes Daddy's car. And although this may seem like simple fun, it is crucial to a child's development. Children reflect on their family life and the things that worry them through games like these.

It's important to give your child an opportunity to develop their imagination, so you should avoid buying them too many electronic games. Dolls or teddy bears, on the other hand can help children channel their frustrations, their desires and their aggression. These toys sometimes serve as a security measure and they help children structure their personalities. Parents should therefore avoid replacing them or even washing them for as long as possible.

What's the Best Way to Play with a Child?

Children often invite adults to join them in their games. "Daddy, you be the robber and I'll be the cop." It is important for us to participate in these games without spoiling the spontaneity of the symbolic play. Try to avoid introducing your own ideas about the games, and let your child's imagination have free rein.

But never use play to hurt their self-esteem or to undermine their sense of self-worth. "Hey Mommy, come have coffee with me!" (The "coffee cups" turn out to be a couple of caps from Coke bottles). You might say, "Well, just look what a delicious cup of coffee you've made!" or "Can I have another cup, and this time with two spoonfuls of sugar. I like mine nice and sweet!" On the other hand, you should never say something like, "Those are bottle caps, not coffee cups, and you should really learn not to use so much sugar."

Try saying, "Okay, you be the teacher and I'll be the student," instead of "I'll be the teacher because I'm a grownup and know more than you do."

When the game is over, tell your child how much fun it was before you bring them back to reality. For instance, you could say, "This has been really fun. Now it's time to put your toys away and get ready to take your bath."

Getting to Know Your Children by Watching Them

We can learn a lot by watching our children. Symbolic play is a window to their inner world. What they do most often gives us an idea about what worries them, and the way they solve problems during play can give us insight into how they resolve conflict. For example, if a child says to their teddy bear, "I'll be home late, but don't cry," we can deduce that parental absences and late arrivals are affecting the child. The invitation to have coffee shows that the child wants to grow up and be just like Mommy, who invites her friends over for coffee. Children imitate the people closest to them—Daddy, Mommy, their grandparents, and their teachers.

Games give children a chance to cope with their feelings and relieve their tension or stress. They provide a sort of release for whatever they have bottled up inside. Ideally, you should provide your children with objects that are not too intricate so they have to use their imagination. That means things like modeling clay, boxes, blocks, paper and pencils, puppets, masks, picture books, and so on.

It is important for children not to spend most of their time watching TV or playing videogames. However, it is normal for children to want to spend most of their time playing. Set some limits and have them alternate between playing and taking care of responsibilities, like taking a bath or helping set the table. A child who does not show any desire to play may be suffering from physical or emotional issues. If that's the case, consult a professional.

HOW TO STOP CHILDREN FROM LYING

When you find out that your son or daughter has lied to you, it can be catastrophic for the parent-child relationship, especially if you had real trust in them. Once your child is caught lying, the trust is broken. You feel betrayed and deceived, and you begin to ask yourself, "What did I do to make my child lie?" You can no longer take their word for it when they say they've finished their homework. "Did they really finish it or is it just time for their favorite TV show?"

Lying is a betrayal that destroys the intimacy between parents and children. It creates mistrust and hinders parents in their role of protecting, advising and guiding.

What should parents do to preserve trust and encourage truthfulness? How can you avoid being aggressive and allow children to have enough privacy and independence to grow and develop a conscience? You don't want to make a federal case out of every little fib, but you also don't want to encourage lying by turning a blind eye to it. Despite the important role that lies play, few parents are aware of how much their own lies influence their children.

"If Aunt Jessica calls, tell her I'm not here…. If Daddy asks what took us so long, tell him there were a lot of people at the store." This is how we unwittingly teach our children to lie. The child thinks, "If Mommy can lie, why can't I?" How can you make a child understand that it's okay for you to lie, but if they do it, they're going to be punished? "How come when I cheat on a test, it's worse than you and Daddy cheating on your income taxes?" an eleven-year-old asks his mother.

The example that parents set is of utmost importance when it comes to learning about lying, but it's not the only factor involved. Other things, like fear of punishment, insecurity, low self-esteem, feelings of belonging, etc. also play a role when children lie.

Fear of Punishment

Nine-year-old Andrew looks away when we ask him about a lie that he told his parents. "If I tell you, are you sure that my parents aren't going to find out?" the little boy asks.

"No," we say, "everything you tell us in therapy is confidential—it's just between you and me."

"I put one of my games in Dad's computer and knocked his keyboard on the floor. Something got disconnected. I knew Dad was going to get really mad. He takes better care of his computer than of himself, and he's told me over and over again not to touch it unless he's with me. So I put the keyboard back and didn't say anything. The next day, he asked, 'Who's been messing with my computer? I can't get it to work!' He asked my brother and my brother said it wasn't him. Then he asked me and I said, 'Not me, I never touched it.'"

Andrew was scared of his father's reaction. In this case, what his father should have said was, "I think somebody touched my computer and accidentally disconnected it. Who was it? Maybe whoever it was can help me figure out how to fix it." When your children tell the truth, compliment them on their honesty, and when the problem is solved, talk to them calmly and say, "See what happens when you play with the computer when I'm not around? I asked you not to use the computer by yourself to keep things like this from happening. When you're older and you've had more practice, you're not going to need me, and you'll be able to use it whenever you want. For now, though, promise me you're not going to use it when I'm not here. I'm trusting your word on this."

When you catch your children in a lie, it is important to ask yourself why they did it. If the answer is that they were afraid of your reaction, then you need to ask yourself, "In the past have I reacted in ways that would make my child afraid of me? Am I punishing them for an accident? Will I make them understand that they have broken a rule?

When children break rules, you need to confront them and show them what the consequences are. But if you do this in an angry way, to punish them, the result won't be educational. Instead, it becomes a way of taking your anger out on the child.

When children feel trusted, they don't go back on their promises. In this case, the parent encourages their child to be good to avoid problems in the future. Stress the good behavior, not the lie. Not overreacting provides your child an incentive to tell the truth. Children often lie because they fear their parents' anger.

Low Self-Esteem

The way you ask the initial question is also important. You should frame the question in a way that encourages your child to tell the truth. Instead of saying "Who broke this glass?" in a voice full of anger, you might say, "We shouldn't have left that glass in a place where it was so easy to knock it over. Who was it, you or your sister? We need to be more careful with fragile things."

Let your children know that they weren't careful today, but that you trust they will be careful in the future, that they'll pay more attention when they handle things, especially things that are at the edge of the table. We need to give children the opportunity to improve and pay more attention. We need to show that we have faith in them.

Pointing a finger directly at the child and saying things like, "You're always so absent-minded, everything falls right out of your hands, you never pay attention," only serves to emphasize these negative behaviors. You're telling the child that they are careless and labeling them. Children start believing what we tell them and they act in accordance with their self-image. Avoid words like "always" and "never," or adjectives like "absent-minded."

Some children lie as a way of boasting, or to raise their status. In cases like these, children will use certain elements of reality, while inventing others. A schoolteacher told us the story of seven-year-old Theresa, who came to school one day wearing a red blouse and told the teacher that everyone in her family was going to wear matching red shirts to her uncle's wedding. She also said her uncle was a waiter at a restaurant, and that he had three jobs. She said that he promised Theresa she could be the godmother of his first child. Several weeks later, at a PTA meeting, the teacher walked up to Theresa's mother and asked, "So how was the wedding?"

"What wedding?" the mother asked. Later she explained to the teacher that her brother hadn't gotten married, he had just moved in with his girlfriend. He only had one job, and at the moment, he and his girlfriend had no intention of having children. Theresa clearly needs attention, to be heard, and that's why she goes to fantastic lengths to make her stories more interesting. She feels that nobody will listen to her if she tells things the way they are. The real problem here is that Theresa isn't getting enough attention at home. She has a number of brothers and sisters, and her parents both work, often arriving home tired. Some children need more attention than others. Although the biggest issue in this case isn't the lying itself, it is important to not let these made-up stories go unnoticed. If she consistently mixes fact and fiction, the little girl may become confused, and start believing her own stories. She might start to think that what happened in her imagination also happened in real life. A lot people carry this problem with them into adulthood.

Lying out of Embarrassment

When five-year-old Olivia gets up from her chair, her mother notices that her pants are wet. "Come here, Olivia," her mother says. "Are your pants wet?"

"I didn't wet them, Mommy," Olivia says. "The chair was wet."

Clearly, Olivia is embarrassed to tell the truth. Sometimes she can't be bothered to stop playing and loses control of her bladder. The real problem here isn't the lie that Olivia told, but the difficulty she has responding to her body's needs. In this case, it's not advisable to draw attention to Olivia's lie or to punish her for it. What is important is to stress the importance of going to the bathroom as soon as she needs to.

When a child lies to hide their embarrassment, give more importance to the reason for the embarrassment than the lie itself.

Why do Some Children Lie more than Others?

The Teachers College of Columbia University in New York has provided an enormous amount of information about children who lie. Their study included 11,000 children from 19 different schools, from grades two through five. The children were induced to cheat on tests and they were also given opportunities to steal money. They were not aware that the researchers knew which of them were lying.

Forty-four percent of the children cheated on tests, and 80 percent of those who cheated lied when asked about it. The question scientists posed was, "Why were some children honest while others lied?" To answer this question, they interviewed the parents in their homes to observe how they interacted with their children.

Researchers found no link between economic status and the tendency to lie. However, the study did show that most of the children who lied also had behavioral issues and difficulty adapting. Also, they engaged in petty theft or were lazy. Lying was frequently found to be associated with fighting, aggressive behavior, and in some cases, drug use. Maladjusted children would break rules and tended to lie in order to avoid punishment.

In further testing, 90 percent of the children who lied showed signs of low self-esteem, and it was observed that they didn't have good relationships with their parents. The study revealed that this behavior stemmed from the inadequate ways in which they were disciplined.

WHICH SIDE OF YOUR CHILD'S BRAIN PREDOMINATES?

When you hear someone described as a logical person, you probably think of someone who is not very emotionally expressive, someone who would rather deal with concrete facts than use their imagination. On the other hand, when you hear someone described as sensitive, you probably assume they get hurt easily or react emotionally if they are pressured or feel uncomfortable. Emotional people can be either introverted or extroverted, but one thing is for sure—they are impressionable, and their mood is what's important. Most of us are somewhere in between emotional and logical, but usually one of the two will predominate.

The same is true of children. For instance, when four-year-old Derek takes away his brother Paul's wagon, Paul's reacts by crying. Then he runs to his mother to express his sadness. A few days later, Derek does it again, this time grabbing a teddy bear that belongs to his cousin Johnny. Johnny, however, immediately sets his sights on Derek's clown doll and plans to "negotiate" a swap—"If you don't give me back my teddy bear, I'm taking your clown," he says. Paul reacts emotionally, while Johnny uses logic. These children cope with life very differently.

Children who react to situations logically tend to favor the left side of their brain. They tend to be more independent when it comes to decision-making and problem-solving. From the moment they start to walk, they want to do everything for themselves, and they relate well to other people and things. They have an investigative spirit and take apart their toys to see how they look on the inside. They are interested in what drives events and things like cause and effect. They like to try things for themselves and arrive at their own conclusions. They tend to be more rebellious and, in general, they need to have their own experiences.

On the other hand, children whose right brain predominates are more interested in human contact and they're more willing to ask for help. They are more dependent on others and it's harder for them to be by themselves. They look for emotional support when they get into difficulties, just like Paul did when he sought refuge in his mother's arms.

It is important for parents to understand their children's character. Left-brained children require precise explanations and guidance to achieve their goals. If you want them to do something, give them a logical explanation. They won't accept things like, "You can't use the phone because I told you so!" Logical explanations, however, won't work with emotional children. It will just make them feel sad that they can't call their friends. Instead, give them a hug, and tell them you understand that they need to talk to their friends, but it would be better for them to see their friends in person the next day. After sharing some quality time with Mommy, the telephone call will no longer seem as important. Emotional children need communication and affection more than they need logical explanations. Left-brained children, meanwhile, may even find the affection irritating.

How you treat your child's achievements should also be different based on what side of their brain predominates. Emotional children need to hear you say that you're proud of them and you value their efforts. "Logical" children are more interested in finding out what they did right and why. Although all children need both praise and explanations of what they did right, the difference is in the order in which you deliver these messages.

Both right and left-brained children are valuable, even if their personality is not in sync with yours. A highly analytical father may get frustrated if his son is too sensitive, and that could make it hard for the two of them to communicate well. Or a highly affectionate mother might feel hurt when her more rational son doesn't respond to her displays of affection. That's why it's so important for parents to figure out what type of character their child has. It will facilitate communication and improve discipline.

After determining whether your child is left or right-brained, it is also important to encourage children to develop the side of their brain that they use the least. Remember, sentimental (right-brained) children still need to connect with logic and objectivity, and rational (left-brained) children still need emotional balance.

Communicating with a Rational Child

- Rational children require explanations and need feelings to be expressed verbally.
- They need help learning to take other peoples' feelings into account.
- It's a good idea to take them to movies that feature emotional things, and to talk to them about their feelings.
- These children enjoy reading about plants and animals. They like science and mathematics.
- Although you should avoid forcing children to be more demonstrative, teach them the importance of communication and affection.
- Rational children are not inclined toward the arts (drawing, painting, music, etc.), and we shouldn't expect them to be.

Communicating with an Emotional Child

- Children who are sensitive need to be treated with love and affection, but don't let them become oversensitive.
- They should be taught logic as well as cause and effect.
- These children tend to be creative and sociable. They have a knack for the arts (drawing, painting, music, etc.).
- Emotional children tend to be untidy. Make sure that they develop good habits.
- Emotional children should be encouraged to be independent and not seek help with every little thing.
- These children enjoy being around their family and good friends.

- Try not to be overprotective with emotional children, because this may hold them back in the future.
- They should be eased into the "real world" and taught about overcoming adversity.

Remember, even within the same family, one child may be rational and the other emotional. It is important for parents to respect and value the differences between their children, avoiding comparisons or making either feel inferior to the other.

Finally, some children use of both sides of their brain equally. If that's the case, it is not necessary to stress the functions of one side or the other. Instead, encourage them to have a wide variety of interests.

WHEN CHILDREN DON'T WANT TO EAT

In the act of suckling, a newborn expresses the will to live. Suckling is an innate instinct and, whether children are breast- or bottle-fed, their first relationship with their mother is established via the mouth. The mother feels a sense of satisfaction when a child drinks all of its milk, and if not, she gets anxious.

Many mothers jump to hasty conclusions and pressure their children to finish their milk. However, lack of appetite may be caused by a wide range of problems, both physical and psychological. In terms of eating, an infant's behavior depends on the relationship they establish with their mother. For example, an anxious mother can cause a baby to lose their appetite. If the child was not "wanted" or "expected" and was born as a result of a "miscalculation" of dates, or because of a failed contraceptive method, the mother may feel a sense of rejection toward the child. And even if she thinks she is hiding it, the child may perceive this feeling in her, especially during the first few months. They may manifest this sense of rejection through lack of appetite. If hunger is an expression of the desire to live, the lack of it expresses the opposite. Of course, we shouldn't generalize. Not all babies lose their appetite because of their mother's emotional state or because they feel rejected. Maybe the child has just woken up and is slow to feed. Or maybe they fall asleep in the middle of feeding. If that's the case, it's not advisable to wake the infant up. It is important to respect the baby's own rhythm.

Anna and Robert are worried because their two-month-old daughter is refusing her milk. She stops suckling and sometimes falls asleep in the middle of breastfeeding. Sometimes, she starts crying before she's finished. But the couple is anxious to show their baby off whenever a family member drops by, so they take the baby out of her crib and gently rock her so she wakes up. "Wait, you've just got to see her eyes! They look just like her father's." The infant bursts into tears and when Ann tries to feed her, convinced that she is hungry, the baby rejects her breast, cries for a while and falls back asleep.

In this case, the parents are not respecting their daughter's rhythm, putting their parental pride before their daughter's needs. Small children require regularity.

It is important to seek the advice of a doctor, especially if the infant is not putting on weight. Weaning a child from the breast is particularly important in a child's development. Weaning should be done little by little. A sudden change can cause the baby to reject the bottle and this can, in turn, diminish their appetite. Remember that the baby is also giving up warm, physical contact with their mother, and still has to get used to a plastic nipple. Also, be careful when the child first starts taking solid food. Give your infant enough time to become accustomed to it, and let them learn chew and swallow in small amounts. At eighteen months, your child will be able to eat at the table with the rest of the family. This change should also be gradual because it involves learning how to use a spoon as well as some behavioral changes. Small children really enjoy sharing the dining experience with their parents and siblings, and you can take advantage of this opportunity to teach them certain rules, like not getting themselves dirty, not throwing food on the floor, not playing with their plate or glass, etc.

When Children won't Eat what they're Served

Molly is nearly three-years old, and for the past two months she has been systematically refusing to eat anything her mother makes for her. Her mother has decided to ask Molly what she would like before preparing meals. "Potatoes or pasta? Apple or banana?" But the problem persists. Once the plate is on the table, regardless of what's on it, the child refuses to eat and asks for something else.

In this case, the issue isn't whether the child wants to eat or not. Rather, it's that Molly has reached the "NO" phase, and allowing her to choose what she wants won't necessarily keep her from rejecting it once it's on the table. When this happens, don't get upset. Instead, deemphasize the child's behavior and say, "I fixed what you asked for. If you don't want to eat it now, that's okay. We'll just put it away for tomorrow. I'm not cooking anything else. You can just go ahead to bed now, and tomorrow you'll have this to eat." The girl probably won't go more than a few nights without her dinner and, after that, she'll get used to eating what she's served. Don't let the child learn to manipulate you when it comes to food, thinking that Mommy is always going to give in to her whims.

There's nothing wrong with respecting children's tastes, but only up to a certain point. They need to get used to eating fruits and vegetables, not just hamburgers and hotdogs. Things that are repeated on a daily basis become habit. For instance, if you never give your children salad, they'll reject it when you do, and say, "I don't like this." Likes and dislikes are a matter of habit. We like what we're used to. We might like rice and beans if we were accustomed to eating that when we were children. And if children eat hamburgers all the time, it might end up being the only thing they'll ever want to eat. Food should be varied, and always include raw fruits and vegetables, which have a high vitamin and mineral content. Also, family habits are of fundamental importance. If children see that their parents don't eat fruits and vegetables, they're not going to like them either. You can't get a child to eat what you don't.

Many children get used to potato chips, cookies or sweets between meals. This can be harmful because it ruins their appetite. Furthermore, this habit is usually the result of anxiety, which children often deal with by eating. Figure out the root cause of their anxiety and, at the same time, place cookies, potato chips and sweets out of their reach.

As for the amount of food that should be served, keep in mind that it depends on their metabolism and the amount of exercise they get. Sometimes parents will force their children to eat more because they fear their kids aren't getting enough to eat. But the fact is that normal, healthy kids will adjust their food intake according to their body's needs. There are no hard and fast rules here. Some children get everything they need from just a little bit of food. You should also watch your child's weight, and consult your doctor if they start losing or gaining too much.

When a child's refusal to eat goes to extremes, they are probably suffering from anorexia nervosa, a mental illness that requires professional treatment. In anorexic children, lack of appetite is accompanied by rapid weight loss. With bulimia, another eating disorder, children will induce vomiting after they eat. Eating disorders are more common among teenagers, whose unresolved childhood issues are more acute.

When Is It Too Much?

Overweight children manifest two types of issues. The first has to do with what is causing them to overeat, and the second has to do with the effects of being overweight.

Once hormonal imbalance has been ruled out, the next crucial step is to investigate the psychological reasons for the child's overeating. It may be caused by nerves, anxiety, or some sort of emotional vacuum that the child tries to "fill with food." Children who lack affection and those that are overprotected both tend to have weight issues. Like adults, they may eat because they are lonely, because they feel unloved, because of anxiety, or because they are lacking other sources of pleasure. The child may say, "Eating is my only pleasure."

Psychotherapy should be used to treat weight problems because it may be indicative of an emotional disturbance. In many cases, it is not the child's fault, and the rest of the family could be contributing to the child's problem. Often, parents are in the habit of snacking between meals, and the child learns this form of anxiety control from them. In such cases, parents may need to start resolving their own issues before expecting their child to resolve theirs.

The Effects of Being Overweight

I'm not going to talk about the physical effects of being overweight here. Although that is a major concern, I'll stick to describing the psychological issues involved. "Chubby" kids are often made fun of by their playmates, who give them nicknames like "Fatty" or "Fatso," etc. Overweight children are often stigmatized, and that makes social integration difficult. This has a profound effect on the child's self-esteem and their performance at school.

If a child's weight isn't brought into balance when they are an infant, it's bound to create problems during their adolescence. Many children dislike eating alone and on a different meal schedule than their parents. Every effort should be made for the family to eat together at least once a day. That provides an enormous benefit not only to children, but to the family as a whole. *The family meal establishes a bond and a very important chance for communication. A calm, pleasant atmosphere whets the appetite and facilitates digestion.*

Don't let the dinner table turn into a battlefield. Remember that eating disorders almost always have an emotional origin. Don't wait until things get complicated. It's important for kids to associate mealtime with an experience of physical contact, communication and harmony. This will help make eating something to look forward to.

I WANT IT NOW!

Some children are very impatient. When they ask for food, water or even a toy, they just can't seem to wait. They become irritable if what they want requires something else to be done beforehand—having to draw the water for their bath, having to change an outfit to go to the park, etc. Cathy, whose daughter is twenty-months old, tells us how she managed to resolve the issue of her little girl's impatience at breakfast time. Her daughter would become very impatient while waiting for breakfast to be prepared. "So I made up the foam game," says Cathy. "As soon as she wakes up, I carry her to the stove area so she can watch how I take milk out of the refrigerator and put it in a pot to boil. While she waits, she keeps a close eye on the milk and when it starts to boil she says, 'It's boiling, it's boiling!' And I sing, "It's boiling, it's boiling," to the tune of a song that she likes, and if it happens to boil over, she giggles and claps her hands. That's how we've turned what used to be a time of stress and crying into an opportunity to have fun together. My little girl wakes up hungry and is very impatient, so I made the game up to help her pass the time while I make breakfast."

Impatience is normal in children—the only experience they have with time is emotional. In fact, it's often the same way for adults, and that's why when we're anxious, the waiting seems endless. That's also why time flies when you're having fun. But through a process of learning and socialization, we acquire a sense of time that is external to ourselves, marked by a clock, not emotion.

For children, the time between asking for something and having their wish granted seems like an eternity, and the younger they are, the more intense this sensation is. Newborn babies want their mother's breast as soon as they wake up. They can't stand to wait a single minute, but little by little, they learn.

Controlling Impatience

Kids have no notion of past or future, and that means your child lives almost entirely in the present, ever attracted by new objects and new situations. Kids don't just want everything they see around them (and right now) they also create images in their minds of other things they'd like to have—the little wagon that Mommy promised or the dessert that Grandma made for after dinner. A vivid imagination makes it difficult for children to wait. It's parents' job to teach them that the world doesn't work that way. It takes more than simply asking for something to have it. It takes time. When it comes to teaching children to wait, attitude is everything. A mom who gets upset when her child cries or yells, but then immediately gives in to their every demand isn't benefiting her child in the least. On the other hand, if you start teaching your children to wait when they are young, they will gradually begin to understand that there is always a waiting period between asking for something and getting it. The worst thing a parent can do is take kids shopping and buy them anything they happen to ask for along the way. That makes children want everything they see, and if they become accustomed to getting anything they want, they will scream and yell and pressure you however they can in order to get it, even when you say no.

If your child asks for something when you're out together, ask them to remind you again when you get home. Let them know you will figure out a good time to buy it.

If your child really wants a particular thing, they'll remind you about it at home, but if not, they will probably forget about it. If they do remind you, tell them that you'll buy it next weekend when you go shopping together. But please, if you say you're going to buy something, keep your word—buy it. Keeping promises is very important to children, and if you don't do it, they might stop trusting what you say. This method will help kids learn that, if they really want something, and you say you'll get it for them, they'll eventually get it, but they will need to wait.

Timing is Everything

Grown-ups tend to use words like "now," "later" or "in a little while" when kids ask us for something. If your child is very young, these kinds of words are meaningless. They're simply too abstract. A more concrete way to describe the passage of time is to connect it to what the child is doing at that moment. Instead of telling your child that a meal will be ready "soon," use their activity to measure time. For example, if they are coloring, try saying, "By the time you're done with your picture, it'll be time to eat." Or if they are doing their homework, you could say, "When you finish your homework, we'll go to the park," or, "You can watch

TV after you take your bath."

When you need to explain an event that will take place much later on, like Daddy's return from a business trip, you can say, "Daddy will be home when you've gone to sleep and gotten up in the morning many times." Something that works well with the younger kids is distraction. If children are itching to go somewhere, instead of telling them to "wait a little while" or "be quiet," talk to them about something else that might interest them, or show them some object that they particularly like. Distraction is effective with kids up to about age three. After that age, you'll have to start explaining the reason for the wait or showing that you understand their eagerness. You might say something like, "I know waiting is hard, but we don't have a choice. We have to wait for your father to get here before we can leave."

Patience is also taught by example, so learn to control your own anxiety and wait calmly. Impatient parents will have a hard time teaching their children to wait. Patience is contagious, and so is impatience—children learn by imitation.

HOW OUR JUDGMENTS AFFECT CHILDREN

"**Y**ou're disrespectful and rude!" says Martha, mother of three, when her youngest one interrupts a conversation she's having with a neighbor—for the fourth time. "I'm getting tired of your interruptions. You don't let me talk!" Lily's mother complains when her daughter interrupts her over and over again.

What is the difference between these two responses? Martha is passing judgment on her child from up above by calling her son "disrespectful and rude." She is directly undermining her child's image of himself. Lily's mother, on the other hand, doesn't act like a judge pronouncing a verdict. She is just conveying her feelings and the effect that her daughter's interruptions are having on her. "I'm getting tired of your interruptions. You don't let me talk!" Lily's mother isn't damaging her daughter's self-image.

The second mother is "teaching" her child how her little girl's interruptions affect her. Her daughter is given the chance to become aware of the negative effect she is having and she, therefore, will be open to change. When parents diminish, judge, embarrass and punish their children, the only thing they achieve is making their child feel unloved, causing them to develop a negative self-image. When this is reinforced on a daily basis with judgmental words like "disrespectful" or "rude," children begin to act in accordance with these labels, and it becomes a part of their self-image.

Therefore, parents need to stop being judges and become "mirrors" that reflect for their children the effects of their actions.

Imagine that you are a child and you're getting the following reactions from your parents. Which of the two would make you feel better?

Parent A

"You're a lazy good-for-nothing. You'll never amount to anything! Just look how tidy your brother is, and you're a mess! Stop pinching Jackson! You're a bad brother! You're heartless!"

Parent B

"I'm worried about your grades! What's going on? Don't you understand your teacher, or is it just that you don't feel like studying? Let's see how I can help you. Listen, I don't want to have to go around picking up after you. And if you keep your area neat, you'll be much more comfortable. It hurts Jackson when you pinch him like that, and he doesn't like it. A nice, smart boy like you can understand that, right? You wouldn't like to have somebody pinching you all the time, would you?"

Parent A's words make the child feel guilty, hurt and attacked. They undermine his self-esteem. Every attack produces a counterattack. The child will probably start interrupting on purpose, being untidy or pinching his little brother to "get even." Judgments produce the opposite effect of what you're seeking and usually don't change your children's behavior. When you judge and label your children, they think that they are their actions: "If I behave badly, I must be a bad person." This is how they gradually form a negative image of themselves.

Meanwhile, the words used by Parent B did not make the child feel personally attacked. Their words let the child know how they feel about their actions and the effects that those actions have.

No child is good all the time. Kids make mistakes during the learning process, and they are always learning. When you equate who your child is with what they do, their self-esteem rises or falls in accordance with their actions, and this keeps kids from developing a sense of self-worth. Even if you don't really believe that your children are bad, that they're not applying themselves, or they're silly, just by hearing these things said, they will believe these labels are really true. And when children form a negative self-image, they begin to feel that they don't deserve anything good.

When girls with low self-esteem become adults, they accept being disrespected, betrayed and undervalued by the men in their lives or at work. They have such a poor self-image that they don't think they deserve better treatment. And when boys with low self-esteem become adults, they often allow themselves to be exploited at work or to be underappreciated by their wives. These men don't make progress in their lives because they don't value themselves and, ultimately, they believe that they deserve it when they suffer because they are "worthless."

How to Avoid Judging Your Child

To avoid being judgmental, talk to your children about the effects of their behavior and how it makes you feel, but do so without resorting to name-calling. You should never use words like lazy, slacker, messy, slow, clumsy, selfish, stingy, shameless, etc. These are words that pass judgment and give children a negative self-image.

Let's take a look at the difference between a parent who judges and one who expresses what they feel and provides instruction on the effects of their child's actions.

Avoid saying things like, "You're always so slow!" or "Don't be such a pig!" or "I don't believe you. You're a liar!" or "Don't be such a bum! Can't you think of anything better to do?"

It is better to say, "I see that you were late for school." or "When you're finished, clean up the crumbs you dropped on the floor." or "I want to be able to take your word for it that you'll do what you say you're going to." or "The reason I'm always talking about the dangers of playing in the street is because I'm afraid something bad might happen to you."

Learning not to be Judgmental

For most of us, learning not to be judgmental is difficult because we've spent our whole lives being judged, and we're used to the judgmental mindset. We think to ourselves, "That's the stupidest thing I've ever heard!" or "What a jerk!" or "This isn't right!" We think, "How dumb of me!" or "This makes me look completely ridiculous!"

To break this habit, we need to start paying attention and catching ourselves when we're passing judgment. And when it happens, we need to swap a judgment for positive action. For instance, when a friend tells you about something they've done, instead of saying, "Wow, you're really gullible!" try saying, "Yes, well, I did something like that once and I was sorry I did."

Try talking about your feelings without passing judgment. To do that, you have to be aware of the problem, be vigilant, and constantly practice breaking the habit. Any effort you make toward this goal will surely be worth it.

The Benefits to Your Children

You may be thinking, "My children are going to be judged and labeled by their friends and teachers, and later on, by their coworkers and bosses." That's true, but if they haven't been burdened by the judgments of people that matter most to them, and if they felt valued during their formative years, they might not pay as much attention to those judgments. They will have formed a positive self-image. Kids who grow up feeling sure of themselves won't feel attacked, and they won't feel the need to attack others.

Children who have positive role-models tend to behave constructively with others and towards themselves. They will grow up self-assured and confident. If they build a good self-image, they'll be successful in everything they set out to do in life. They'll have high self-esteem, and if they value themselves, other people will value them too.

HOW TELEVISION AFFECTS CHILDREN

"Thanks to a new apparatus, television, now families can stay together in a single room" (*The New York Times*, 1949). "With the advent of television, the gap between parent and child has been eliminated" (*The New Yorker*, 1949). Comments like these came at a time when families were giving a warm welcome to a new invention—television. Back then it was impossible to understand the full effect of this "new guest" in people's homes, and no one knew how much it would distort communication among family members, or even that someday, people would have more than one TV in their home. It was impossible to foresee how television would change the way people spent their free time, or that it would affect children's ability to socialize, or the amount of violence in our society.

No one could have predicted that television would wreak havoc in terms of family communication, but the reality is that in many homes, the only time the family ever gets together is at mealtimes. Even then, the TV is on while the family is silent. TV has upset the way we organize our system of living together on a daily basis—the rituals in which each member of the family has a specific role. For instance, meals, bedtime, vacation, weekends, and so on.

Some parents tell their kids to go watch TV so they'll stop fighting with each other. Maybe they think that instead of teaching them to resolve conflicts, it's better for them to escape reality by watching something on television. But when conflict between siblings doesn't get resolved, resentment starts to build, and sooner or later it is bound to be manifested. Young adults spend many hours away from home, separated from their parents, yet when they get back, they spend hours more without exchanging a word. Instead, they watch television. And sometimes parents are the ones watching their favorite TV program, not letting their children speak. Then it's time for dinner, where the only sounds are knives and forks on plates and the blood-curdling screams of a woman being murdered on TV. And after that, it's off to bed so the same scene can be repeated the next day. Little by little, family members become strangers to each other. Parents only intervene to say, "Don't do this or that. Don't be rude. You should be getting better grades at school," and so on. Children get the feeling that their parents are only there to scold, threaten and tell them what they can and can't do, and little by little, they learn to tune their parents out, to stop listening or responding when they're spoken to. They start thinking: "Why should I? They're just going to tell me what to do or that I'm doing something wrong." More and more, they turn up the volume and end up more connected to the TV screen than to the world around them.

Thanks to television, mothers can keep their children quiet, fathers can avoid hearing their wives complain, and conflicts can be swept under the rug so that everything appears to be fine. Fine, that is, until mother finds out that her child has stopped going to school or is using drugs, and then she can't fathom what possibly could have happened. She may even say, "Everything was fine in this family until that happened." But that's not where the problem started. When a young person drops out of school or starts using drugs, it is the result of a process that began years earlier, not when the problem is just coming to light. But no one saw it coming because there was no communication, and when conflicts arose, the family drowned them out with TV instead of resolving them.

"I'm Bored!"

"Why can't my son think of anything better to do than sit around and watch TV?" asks a young mother. This is the dilemma parents find themselves in every time they decide to turn off the television. Kids can't find anything to do and their parents can't stand seeing them hanging around the house doing nothing and whining as if their lives were over. Television has become a replacement for the effort that parents were forced make in the past to entertain their children. Without those hours watching TV, you end up actually having to spend time with them, take them to the park, read stories to them, play a board game with them. Or you have to listen to your teenager's problems, which you may not be sure how to fix. Parents need to be prepared for this, because without television, children don't know how to entertain themselves. Parents need to give children the time they need to learn how to make good use of their free time, to develop their capacity for play. Children need to learn how to play the way we did, like by pretending a broomstick was a sleek, beautiful horse. You can't expect your children to suddenly develop a strong imagination and unique creative abilities if they spend their spare time staring at a TV screen.

One three-year old child's mother says, "Danny spends hours on end watching television. I don't know if he understands everything he sees, but what worries me is that he hardly talks. He mostly just points at what he wants. It seems like other kids his age are a lot more talkative." If your child is a pre-schooler and spends many hours in front of the TV, be careful! Among other things, this can affect their ability to acquire language.

To understand this, we need to delve into the nature of language and how it is acquired and developed. The cerebral cortex is divided into two parts called cerebral hemispheres, each of which has its own functions. The right hemisphere controls movements on the left side of the body, and vice versa. The left hemisphere controls logic, mathematics and language, while the right deals with spatial, visual, creative and intuitive abilities.

The right side of the brain is highly activated in a creative, artistic person, while the left side is more developed in mathematicians. Experience is what makes each cerebral hemisphere evolve and activate, and our school system tends to stress left-hemisphere development. When someone has an accident that damages the left side of their brain, they will start to have difficulty with language and mathematical reasoning, and if the accident victim is an adult, they can also lose the ability to speak. If the accident damages the right hemisphere of the brain, the victim could lose the ability to recognize other people or their sense of touch. Their language ability will not be affected, however.

The human brain possesses two basic types of intelligence: verbal-mathematical and spatial-visual. A sketch artist's right brain is more developed, while the left brain is the more developed in a chemist. The cerebral hemisphere that is more highly developed will be dominant, and it will determine your skill and talents. Verbal thought starts to develop when a child is one year old. That's when children begin to combine the use of both hemispheres, with a visual stimulus causing a verbal response.

When children who are pronouncing their first words watch too much TV, it can put the left side of the brain to sleep, while overstimulating the right side. This can cause a child to be slower to acquire linguistic logic and mathematical reasoning. Many renowned linguists like Noam Chomsky maintain that by the age of two, children should be receiving stimuli that demand a verbal response. Without adults to expect or demand a verbal response from them, children may become slow to grasp language, which puts them at a disadvantage to other children their age. Television is a "unidirectional" communications system. It does not demand a response from the viewer, and it, therefore, reinforces laziness and dulls the imagination, logic and verbal skills.

TV and Play

Ever since the advent of television, children feel less like exploring, creating and working to reach a goal. Their imaginations have been weakened. Playing motivates children to explore the world around them. They instinctively want to play with things and figure out what they like and what they don't, as well as their strengths and weaknesses. Television, on the other hand, leads to passivity and inactivity. By playing, children learn to enjoy things and share them. Most of all, they learn to value and consider the feelings of other people. When kids sit in front of a TV, they aren't communicating—not even when their siblings are sitting right next to them. The television robs them of the opportunity to learn to communicate and get to know the people around them. This makes them egocentric and they start being intolerant of other children.

Gradually, children who play construct an elaborate system of communication with the objects around them. They invent new situations and new solutions to problems. On television, though, the answers have already been provided for them, and the new situations have been created by someone else. Curiosity comes into play when a child feels the urge to explore and learn. Indeed, television might arouse their curiosity, but only for as long as the child is "connected" to the screen. On the other hand, it tends to diminish children's curiosity in other areas of daily life, where they have to exercise their logic, memory, and creative imagination, and move around physically.

Television and Violence
A report by the American Psychology Association (APA) reveals that the average American child has seen 8,000 murders and 100,000 other acts of violence on TV by the time they finish elementary school. The study claims that violence on television has an especially strong influence on young children and teens, and may encourage them to use aggression to resolve conflict.

We can't, however, place all the blame on TV networks. After all, they air what people want to see. They know that if they put an educational program on instead of a violent and sexual movie, their ratings will drop. But this means that if we changed channels or turned the TV off every time a violent movie came on, we would force the networks to provide more educational content.

What should you do? The best solution is for parents to be selective about what programs their children watch and reduce the amount of time in front of the TV. Spend more time talking and playing with your children, and if you have to go to work, make sure that whoever is taking care of them doesn't just plant them in front of the TV "to keep them out of trouble."

And buy a few board games, like chess, backgammon, monopoly, etc, for those winter days when you can't go outside.

HOW TO HELP CHILDREN WITH LEARNING DIFFICULTIES

There are several important decisions a parent has to make when they discover that their child has learning difficulties. First, they need to decide whether they even believe the diagnosis. They might not want to rely solely on the judgment of one particular expert, and they may want a second opinion. Sometimes parents can't handle the news that their child suffers from learning difficulties and they refuse to accept what the experts tell them, but keep in mind that until they do, nothing can be done to help their child. It will be impossible to make the adjustments that they need, both at home and in school, unless parents clearly understand the nature of the child's problem. Only then can parents take action.

The second step is to ask yourself, "If my child has learning issues, what can I do to help?" Some parents try to keep their child's learning difficulty a secret, or they simply act like it doesn't exist. They seem to think that if they ignore the problem, it will go away on its own. Others may go to the opposite extreme. The child's issues become the central focus of the family. Keep in mind that both ignoring the problem and paying an exaggerated amount of attention to it are equally counterproductive.

Many parents are reluctant to place their child in special education classes or to send them to therapy.

In a regular classroom, children with learning difficulties tend to get made fun of by their classmates, and a sense of failure and frustration takes root in them, creating severe behavioral issues like withdrawal, isolation, extreme loneliness and feelings of unhappiness. Often this reaches the point where the child no longer wishes to go to school. Nevertheless, when a teacher informs parents that their child will be sent to a special education class, and that they should have therapy, parents sometimes react by saying that their son or daughter is just being picked on. Just as parents have to learn to accept the fact that their child has a learning difficulty, the child must also learn to live with this reality. As long as they remain in a regular classroom without receiving any kind of special help, that child is going to feel inferior, that they "can't do" what the other kids can. If the child fails to understand that they have a learning difficulty, their self-esteem will suffer. Yet, children who understand that they have an issue that can be overcome with proper treatment will be more willing to cooperate. They won't feel that they are "stupid" or less valuable than anybody else, and they will be able to start resolving an issue that is not their fault.

Urging a child to hide the truth from themselves and others is no way to help. The first step is to help children with learning difficulties understand that their issues can be resolved if they are willing to do their part—by allowing specially-trained individuals to help. Remember, if you don't acknowledge a problem, you can't solve it.

One of the first things parents have to do is find out whether the origin of their child's learning difficulty is emotional or physiological. A psychologist should be able to determine that by running a series of tests. If it is physiological, the child can be referred to a neurologist or another specialist. Remember that the sooner the cause of the learning difficulty is discovered, the faster it can be dealt with. If children with learning difficulties don't get help early enough, their issues can become chronic—for them, their parents and for society.

It's usually fairly easy to tell if a child has a learning difficulty (also known as "LD") although there are also special tests designed to detect it. Often, a teacher will send a child to be evaluated by a specialist within the school system. Unfortunately, once these evaluations are completed, many parents resist taking their children to therapy, especially when they aren't sure what it actually involves, or if they doubt the reliability of the evaluator or the teacher. If parents decide to ignore the situation, thinking their child will simply outgrow it, all they are doing is delaying treatment and making matters worse. It can even get to the point where the child loses all interest in study, eventually coming to believe that their difficulties are insurmountable. Ultimately, when parents are reluctant to take their children with LD to therapy, they are making a decision about their child's future. The longer it goes unchecked, the worse the learning difficulty will get. When children feel inferior to their classmates, their self-esteem is undermined and that could eventually cause them to do things like drop out of school. And we all know the rest of the story—no job opportunities and constantly feeling inferior to others. These children have trouble finding the right partner, since low self-esteem leads them to be with other people who feel inferior, which in turn, only confirms their belief that they are worthless. These situations can be avoided by taking immediate action, and seeking a solution as soon as the learning difficulty is detected. Remember, learning difficulties can be treated.

Below is a description of the most common symptoms found in children with LD, but keep in mind that a child may present one or more of these symptoms. Furthermore, a very young child may present several of these symptoms without actually having a learning difficulty. Only a qualified professional can provide an accurate diagnosis. LD has nothing to do with a child's intelligence. Nor does the number of symptoms indicate whether the learning difficulty is severe or mild. Only a professional can determine the magnitude of the problem.

Confusion with Directions

Many children with LD have problems differentiating between left and right (although this should only be considered in children over five). If asked which way they should go, they may point in the right direction, but hesitate when asked if that is left or right. If you say to a child with LD, "Touch your left eye," they will have trouble deciding which is which and won't even be sure after they've made a choice. Adults who have suffered from learning difficulties are sometimes embarrassed when they continue to confuse left and right. Many people simply learn to live with this annoyance and compensate for it in other ways. For example, Sally, 28, always wears her watch on her left wrist and looks at it before answering any questions about directions.

Frequently, confusion with directions is observed in several members of the same family. And it's also common to find more than one case of undetected and untreated LD in the same family.

Difficulty Recalling Sequences

Some people with LD may have problems remembering things in order. In kindergarten a child may have a hard time memorizing the alphabet. By second or third grade, most children can remember the months of the year, but a child with LD won't be able to recite them in the right order. Adults with this issue can remember telephone numbers, but when they have to say them out loud, they might switch the digits around.

Slow Speech Development

Some children with LD learn to speak later than others. And these children may continue to use baby talk until they are quite grown. Others may lisp or have difficulty pronouncing certain letters. One woman who visited our office told us, "My son didn't start talking until he was three years old, but since then it's become impossible to make him stop." Later, when the child was in the fifth grade, the teacher told his mother that the boy didn't read as well as he should, especially considering that he was very intelligent. This early symptom of LD manifested itself as slow development of speech. It was not detected early on, and since the child eventually started speaking, the parents thought that there was nothing to worry about. Then the problem re-emerged in the form of reading difficulties.

Difficulty Telling Time

Many people reach adulthood ashamed of the fact that they can't tell time by a conventional analog clock. And by the time some children reach the sixth or seventh grade, they have developed a wide array of methods to cover up the fact that they don't know the difference between nine o'clock and a quarter past six. Many only wear digital watches, or they simply don't wear watches at all and ask other people what time it is. Sometimes, people think that those who have difficulty telling time are just acting silly or "lying." Some children over the age of five have trouble telling the difference between the concepts of *before* and *after*, or *early* and *late*. Most of us have a natural, built-in sense of time that allows us to estimate when an hour (give or take) has gone by, and to tell the difference between ten minutes and one hour. But some people with LD have no "inner clock" and struggle to perceive the passage of time. Many wear a watch but forget to look at it. It's not unusual for children to complain when they are told it's bedtime, but those with LD are particularly defiant. It often helps for parents to give these children a five-minute warning beforehand.

Problems with Verbal Expression

Many children with LD have trouble expressing themselves. They have an idea of what they want to say, but don't know how to express it. These kids may have trouble defending themselves in an argument and tend to react physically. Many times, when they can't express their anger in words, they hit others. Such children can be easily misinterpreted, and this causes frustration. They may be able to read a text, but they'll have trouble answering questions about its content, even if they have understood it correctly. They grow up having a lot of conflict in their relationships with adults and other children. They need to be treated with a lot of patience—the problem can often be overcome with appropriate therapy.

Poor Motor Skills

These are the kids who trip over everything in their path, and sometimes, even over their own feet. They have trouble catching a ball and are usually left out when other kids choose sides for games because of their lack of coordination. Eight-year-old Karen still spills her milk at the table. That makes her mother very angry, and despite being punished for it, Karen keeps doing it. She is convinced that she does this completely unintentionally and that she can't control certain sudden movements she makes with her arms. In cases like this, it is helpful for kids to have physical activities like swimming or tennis. Many children who demonstrate a lack of control over their larger muscle groups (arms and legs) don't have any problems with precision movements like using a ruler, drawing or handwriting.

Attention Issues

Many children with LD have a very short attention span and constantly skip around from one thing to another. They can't focus for long periods of time, they are easily distracted, and any noise or movement might "disconnect them" from what they are doing. These children have trouble isolating themselves from what's going on around them. In cases like this, parents need to organize a quiet place away from the rest of the family where their child can do their homework. Have your child's desk facing a wall and away from any windows. It's important to avoid distraction. Also, you can stimulate your child's mind with games that help develop concentration. Therapy for attention and concentration difficulties usually provides excellent results.

Hyperactivity

Hyperactive kids can't stay still in their seats. They can't stop moving, walking around and jumping up and down. This is an issue that should be treated before your child starts feeling rejected by adults and developing low self-esteem. Hyperactive children understand that their inability to sit still negatively affects grownups. Therapy can provide some positive changes.

Poor Reading Skills

"Lucy could read perfectly well if she just paid more attention," her mother tells us. And indeed, it seems surprising that Lucy, who is five years old, is very capable of reading long, difficult words like "something" or "whatever," while getting tripped up on easy words like "to," "when" and "out," which are so important in putting together a sentence. This problem is common in children with LD. At age nineteen, Jack discovered that although he was good at reading to himself, he made so many mistakes when he had to read out loud, that the text would become unintelligible. Nevertheless, it seemed as if Jack had a decoder in his head because whenever he read to himself, he was somehow able to rearrange the words in his mind so that he understood every word. Many kids with LD reach the seventh or eighth grade and never raise their hands to ask the teacher a question. They're afraid their problem will be revealed. Over time they learn to hide their learning difficulty so their classmates won't make fun of them. Sometimes a child wants to write "he," but instead writes "she." When that happens, they become furious with themselves and start distrusting their own hand. They instruct their hand to write one thing, but it writes something else. This can cause kids to get extremely upset, break into tears, throw tantrums, throw their pencil, or rip the page into a thousand pieces.

Inability to Copy

"How do you write 'remember?'" a child asks. Her teacher writes the word on the board, and her mother spells it out. Nevertheless, the child writes it with an "n" instead of an "m." "All you have to do is copy it off the board, and you can't even do that right!" the child's mother complains.

But a child with LD is going to make mistakes when they down words, and no amount of scolding is going to change that. The child suffers and feels ashamed but can't overcome the problem. Many parents think that it's just a matter of practice, and that if their child recopies the same sentence enough times, they'll get better at it. But the problem persists—there are people who graduate from college and continue having difficulty copying texts. Special therapies are designed for this issue.

Poor Spelling

Spelling issues are very difficult to overcome. A person with LD may have difficulty remembering sequences, the order of the letters, and the way a word it written. There are people who reach adulthood, who have seen a word like "receive" or "believe" hundreds of times, but can't seem to remember whether it is written with an "ie" or an "ei." There are specific therapies for this, and of course, good reading habits help a lot.

Problems with Written Expression

Often people with learning difficulties are perfectly capable of holding an intelligent conversation, speaking clearly and with good pronunciation. Nonetheless, they can't effectively express themselves in writing. When asked to write a composition, many children say that they "don't know what to write." These kids hate having to write anything for school, and they get writer's block every time they're asked to do it. Even if these children know what they want to say, the ideas evaporate when it comes time to put them on paper.

Hostile and Aggressive Children

Kids with learning difficulties who don't receive help may become hostile, aggressive or introverted. When children can't do their schoolwork they feel frustrated. They find other activities to occupy their time, like tossing paper airplanes, leaving their seats, getting up for a drink of water, or simply daydreaming. With proper therapy and a little understanding from their parents, they are not going to experience the intense anger and pain caused by failure. They won't be pushed to the point of mental illness. And they won't have to cope with accusations of being "lazy" or "absent-minded."

HOW TO PREPARE YOUR CHILDREN FOR HEALTHY SEXUALITY

Why Is Teaching Sex an Issue?

If sex education just meant teaching kids how to have sexual relations, it would be easy enough for parents to sidestep their responsibilities. They could simply buy their children a book and leave it up to the school system to take care of the rest. But it is their attitude toward sex which determines how young men and women deal with their sexuality.

In reality, parents should be teaching their children these attitudes—respect for sexuality and for oneself. And learning these attitudes begins when the child is still a baby. How does one have a sexual relationship? Technically speaking this question,, is actually of minor importance because a young person can get this information from any of a number of books or by having a simple conversation with their parents.

It's true that this is the twenty-first century, but

lingering beneath the surface in many of us are beliefs handed down from previous generations—beliefs that foster the idea that sex is something bad or dirty. We were brought up in an environment where the topic of sex was considered taboo. Nobody talked about it, especially not our parents. Most of us just don't have any experience talking to our children about sexuality. We don't have a point of reference.

During the fifteenth and sixteenth centuries, sex was considered sinful and was accepted only as a means of preserving the species. Enjoying sex was considered the work of the devil, and even between married couples, it was considered uncivilized or savage. For women in particular, enjoying sex was thought to be immoral and dirty. Of course, everybody was doing it, but clandestinely, out of sight, and full of repressed feelings and guilt. The fact that sex gets an exaggerated amount of attention today is just a reaction to the fact that it was kept hidden and repressed for so many centuries. Social behavior swings like a pendulum. It shifts from one extreme to the other until it eventually settles in the middle. After being hidden from view for so long, sex has burst onto the scene everywhere— on television, advertisements, restaurants, movies, the arts and fashion.

But sex deserves our respect. There must be some sort of middle ground where it is neither kept hidden nor exaggeratedly displayed. It should be associated with love, responsibility and commitment, and it should nourish and enrich human relationships. It should never be used as a means of getting power over others or controlling them, and it should never lead to self-destructive behavior or a lack of self-respect. Sex misused can destroy human relationships as well as our self-esteem.

The way teenagers handle their sexual impulses is

connected to their experiences with life and love from the time they are born.

Sex and Love

It was long thought that the urge to procreate and find a mate was instinctive, but further observation appears to indicate that these so-called "instincts" are the product of learning. Female monkeys who are separated from their mothers at birth tend to show little interest in breeding when they reach adulthood. They also tend to reject their young.

Some research indicates that the adult sexual drive is colored by the physical displays of affection, the tenderness and human contact we receive during infancy. In order for human beings to give love, we have to have received it, and every time you hug, rock, bathe or feed your baby, you are providing them with that experience of receiving love. A person's ability to enjoy intimate relationships when they become adults is determined by these parental expressions of affection. Warmth and tenderness and showing respect for a child's body constitute an infant's first exposure to love and physical contact—this is where sex education begins. When you provide your children with trust and self-esteem, and when you pay attention to them without passing judgment, you teach them communication, intimacy and commitment. You teach them that opening up emotionally to people who are important in their lives is nurturing, not dangerous. Children who feel rejected when they need physical contact tend to find intimate contact of any kind risky and, as adults, they will seek physical contact without any emotional exchange or real affection.

Sexual contact is always more satisfying when it occurs within the context of tenderness, affection and sensitivity for the other person's interests. Sex is also more satisfying when it is accompanied by commitment, trust and security. Young people who have grown up in an atmosphere of security, communication and trust are more likely to nurture these types of feelings in their sexual relationships, and they'll have less interest in purely recreational sex.

Children repress their emotions if they are not allowed to express them. "Stop your whimpering! How dare you get angry with me. I'm your mother! Don't talk to me about how you feel. If I yell at you, and it hurts your feelings, too bad! You deserve it!"

Children suffer in silence when they hear their parents fighting constantly, and when they see their father physically or emotionally abusing their mother, they store up their pain—and this also leads them to repress their feelings. During the teenage years, sex can become a relief valve for repressed emotions. It becomes an urgent need, an uncontrollable impulse through which these repressed emotions are unburdened.

Many adult men will use sex as an outlet for their negative feelings. Ted, 35, frequently "took revenge" on his wife when he was under a lot of pressure. He would reach orgasm quickly, before she could, leaving her frustrated and angry. This "payback" was an unconscious tactic, but it was a powerful one. When couples avoid conflict and don't talk out their problems, or when they repress their rage and their frustrations—they often find an outlet in sex. Sexual dysfunction and low libido are usually symptoms of repressed feelings and communication issues. When parents resolve conflict through open dialogue with one another, and when they encourage their children to vent their emotions, too, they are giving their children healthy sex education. When they grow up, children who are brought up this way won't use sex as an escape valve for their repressed feelings. They'll be capable of expressing their emotions with words.

Gender Identification and its Role

Nothing is more devastating to a boy or girl than feeling that their gender makes them inferior to others. It destroys their self-esteem.

Mr. Martin was convinced that his firstborn would be a boy, and he spent hours on end planning the things he would do with his future son. When the long-awaited child was finally born, it turned out to be a girl, who they named Samantha. But her father insisted on calling his daughter "my little guy." Samantha never felt comfortable with herself. She felt that she had disappointed her father by being born a female. As a result, she began to take on male postures and attitudes—unconsciously, as a way to ingratiate herself with her father. She always felt more comfortable when she hung out with other boys because of this lack of identification with her female side. When Samantha's sexuality began to awaken, she was attracted to girls, and soon she realized that she was a lesbian.

When parents resent their child's gender, they should analyze themselves, figure out why and take active steps to control the way they feel. If they don't do this, their child isn't going to feel comfortable with their gender. Also, parents should not allow themselves to demonstrate a gender preference. This could make their children feel rejected and affect on their self-esteem.`

Attitudes toward Sex

A boy who has been overly dominated and controlled by his mother will tend to use his sexuality to control women, using it as a form of "revenge." As an adult, a child like this tends to turn the sex act into something more like rape than like something pleasurable for two individuals.

For him, a woman is "someone who I must crush and dominate before she starts controlling me."

Many young women use sex as a substitute for affection. They have sexual relations with a number of boys in the search for the love and affection they lacked as little girls. If the girl's father has been overly domineering, the young woman may adopt a manipulative and controlling attitude toward men, to prevent them from dominating her the way her father did. A young woman will probably use sex to get the emotional and material support she was lacking if her father failed to satisfy her emotional and material needs when she was a young girl. "I surrender myself sexually in exchange for affection and material security." Sex, then, becomes a way of getting what she needs.

When sex is taboo and "we don't talk about those things," children try to satisfy their natural curiosity by getting the information they want from friends or schoolmates. Or through pornographic magazines or videos that only manage to "warp" their ideas of what healthy sexuality is. Sexuality can't be ignored in a society that bombards us with sexual imagery. If you have a hard time discussing this subject with your children, it may help to go to the public library to find books and videos that can help you broach the topic. It can be daunting to talk to a teenager about sex when you've never had that conversation before, so you should start when your child is three or four years old, which is when they usually start asking where babies come from. Human beings begin to awaken their sexuality at that age, so it's a normal question. That's when little boys and girls start getting interested in the difference between their genitalia. It's the age when they start "playing doctor," when girls and boys start wanting to see each other. If parents satisfy their child's normal curiosity, they won't keep insisting on the subject. However, consult a professional if excessive interest or frequent masturbation is observed. If questions about sexuality are answered naturally, as if talking about any other subject, children with feel confident enough to continue asking questions whenever their curiosity is aroused. But if these kinds of questions are met with evasive responses like "Ask your father," or "You'll understand when you're older," your child will stop asking you. Instead, they'll get their answers elsewhere.

If a child's first questions about sexuality are met with embarrassment, anger or jokes, children get the message not to ask about it. Statistics show that girls and boys who receive sexual information at home start having sexual relations at a later age. Curiosity is not what drives them to start having sexual relations when they are young. Teenage girls compensate for their lack affection and communication at home by seeking what seems like intimate, emotional relationships, but which are actually devoid of those things.

Human beings go through life compensating. When we lack something, we try to make up for it with something else. Why is it that we can talk about so many other things, but when it comes to sexuality, which forms an integral part of our lives, it's just so difficult? We've learned that it's bad and dirty, and we feel guilty about it. Nowadays, if you're stuck on those old ways of thinking, you will be putting the health, welfare and emotional balance of your children at risk.

When children are sexually abused, it is usually by a family member, neighbor or friend. Children start tolerating dangerous caresses because no one ever told them it's not appropriate. Usually when something like that happens, children hide it because they're scared, because "we don't talk about that sort of thing." Most sexually-abused children don't have enough information and they don't discuss sex with their parents. *Talking to your children about their sexuality is the best way to protect them.*

LEFT OR RIGHT HAND?

Our society places a lot of value on right-handedness. In the Middle Ages it was the hand that held the sword. We shake hands with our right hand. Dexterous (from the Latin *dexter*, or right-handed) means skillful, while up*right* means honorable, loyal and strong. In contrast, the word sinister comes from the Latin root meaning "left-handed," and it means perverse and sneaky. In English, the word right comes from the Old English *riht*, meaning just, good and fair, while left is from the Old English *lyft*, meaning weak or foolish. In India, they eat with their right hand and use the left for the things they consider impure. In the religious art of the Sistine Chapel, Christ assigns his right side to the just and his left side to sinners. For centuries, right has been associated with all that is good, and left with all that is bad.

We've grown up our whole lives with these ideas of good and bad, so sometimes we become intolerant when we see our child favoring their left hand, and we subconsciously pressure them to use their other hand. "Everything in this life is made for right-handed people," some parents argue. "Think about it: cars (with the exception of England), guitars, typewriters and other tools." But thanks to the progress that has been made in psychology in recent years, we understand that there is no need to change left-handed children. Nowadays, it's clear that they can do just about anything that right-handed children can, even when using implements made for their right hand. We now know that there are no good reasons not to let your child use the hand they prefer.

Most infants pick up their toys with the same hand, and roughly by the age of four, they are fully proficient with it. By that age, even left-handed children can use scissors without much difficulty. And there are scores of ambidextrous people (who are equally skilled with both hands). Only when these children learn to write are they forced to make a choice. Some choose to write with their right hand, but use their left to draw and paint, or hold a tennis racket.

It's a very simple situation, as long as adults don't get involved. Unfortunately, parents sometimes pressure their left-handed children with authoritarian methods that can make their children feel ashamed. But aside from undermining their self-esteem and their sense of self-worth by making them feel like there is something wrong with them, parents run the risk of impairing their child's hand-eye coordination when they demand that their children use their right hand.

When a child is left-handed, this is an indication that their "right-brain" predominates. In addition to controlling the left side of the body, the right side of the brain is the origin of our creativity, emotion, intuition and our aesthetic sense. The left lobe of the brain governs the right side of the body and controls logic, mathematics, and language. Therefore, left-handed children tend to be more intuitive, sentimental and creative. They tend to be interested in the arts, they're good at drawing or music, and they have a creative imagination. By restricting their left-hand, parents may also be affecting their children's innate talents.

Left-handed children tend to have more difficulty with mathematics and things that requires rigorous thinking. That doesn't mean they can't acquire those skills, but it might require more attention from their parents and teachers. If your child has difficulty with these subjects, you should seek more information, so you can give them the extra help they need. There are various things that parents can do with their children to stimulate the left side of their brain and facilitate the learning process for math, the sciences, reading and writing.

The mother of a six-year old child who is just beginning to write, tells me, "He picks up his pencil with his left hand, but I'm convinced he is right-handed. There's never been a lefty in my family or in my husband's. His teacher doesn't seem to care." For his age, the boy is short and timid, too. He doesn't say a word. But when he takes the evaluation tests, it turns out that he is, in fact, left-handed. The child is anxious to write with his right hand, and rather embarrassedly, he says, "My left hand is bad. It wants to do everything, and my right hand is bad, too, because it can't do anything right."

This little boy is trapped between a mother who considers left-handedness abnormal and bad, and a teacher who hasn't been paying attention to the situation. Who should he listen to? Which hand should he choose? Who's right? The boy is upset and embarrassed, and he thinks there's something wrong with him that he can't control. This makes him shy around other people—he is ashamed of himself. He is insecure and lacks self-worth. He may grow up with all of the consequences of low self-esteem: lack of motivation, insecurity, a tendency to underachieve, etc.

In the old days, teachers often tried to force left-handed children to use their right hand. And until not too long ago, it was common for them to hit their left hand with a ruler or force them to keep it under their desk. Today, however, we know that this is counterproductive and that we should respect the child's natural tendencies. Be aware that left-handed children can be successful in life, and they can even adapt to some activities using their right hand.

Some kids use their left hand to imitate their parents.

Four-year-old Eric has asked his mother to help him write his name. She writes the letters on a page and the child copies them. A few days later, she sees Eric with the pencil in his left hand, when, previously, he was using his right. His mother points it out, but Eric denies it, saying, "I want to do it like Daddy." Eric's mother is right-handed, but his father is a lefty. Eric has deduced that men are left-handed and women are right-handed, and his mother is having a hard time convincing him that it has nothing to do with gender. This logic is common for a four-year-old boy. He identifies with his father and wants to emulate him. He is at the age when a boy becomes aware that he is male, like his father. In this case, writing with his left hand will most likely be just a phase, since the child is actually right-handed. Sooner or later, he'll realize that it's easier for him to use his right hand.

Left-handed children often become artists, designers, actors, musicians, and successful businesspeople who make decisions intuitively.

HOW TO HELP CHILDREN DEVELOP
SELF-CONFIDENCE

Mark is beside himself with rage. His mother shouts, "Go to your room and stay there until you've cooled off!" She is letting him "own" his irritation and become conscious of his feelings, but she is also letting him know that she doesn't want to speak to him while he's in that state.

Much of the tension in families is caused by negative emotions, but if Mark's mother had allowed herself to "take the bait" and shout back, it would have caused a war of words. Teenagers and preteens get irritated or upset at the drop of a hat, and that would have escalated the situation.

It's essential to recognize that children have feelings. Sometimes they get anxious, confused, out of sorts, and they need to feel protected. They need understanding and acceptance. Think about how it feels when you want to express an emotion and share it with another person. You need to feel understood and not have someone tell you how you should feel. It makes you feel secure, and it motivates you to keep talking. If you feel uneasy because your child is sick and you tell a friend about it, you're not going to feel understood if they say, "Don't worry, it's not a big deal, kids get sick all the time." Instead of feeling relieved, you'll probably be thinking, "She doesn't have kids. She doesn't know how a mother feels. I won't be discussing my worries with her anymore. She doesn't understand me." But it's a whole different story if your friend says, "This must be really tough on you. You should take your child to another doctor, get a second opinion so you won't have to worry. *I know how you feel. I know what must be going through your head right now.*"

These words indicate that your friend understands how you feel. When you express your concerns or your fears to someone, you're looking for understanding and support— you don't want to be judged or to have somebody tell you that what you're feeling is unreasonable. It's not good to have somebody tell you that you shouldn't be feeling a certain way. *When people understand what we're going through, it comforts us and makes us feel secure.*

But don't confuse understanding with pity. When someone says, "Oh, you poor thing!" that doesn't make you feel more understood, either. It only shows that someone feels sorry for you. Pity from others doesn't help or make you feel secure. There's a word for the understanding that all of us yearn for: EMPATHY.

But, never confuse **empathy** with **sympathy**. Empathy means being understood from your own point of view. It means that someone has momentarily "put themselves in your shoes." It means someone has managed to penetrate your world and feel what you feel. For a short time, someone has left their own point of view behind to "be with you."

Paying Attention to Body Language

If you want to be more empathetic, it's important not only to listen to people's words, but also to pay attention to their body language. If Johnny comes into the room with his head down and shoulders hunched and says with a sad voice, "I'm finished with my math homework," his words are telling you that his homework is finished, but his tone of voice and demeanor show that he's feeling dejected and discouraged. If his father robotically responds without even taking his eyes off the TV, saying "so, you're all finished, that's great," Johnny will feel that at some level, he's not being entirely understood. Johnny's feelings about his homework are more important than whether he's done it, but his father has disregarded those feelings. On the other hand, if his father had paid real attention to the entire message, including his body language, he'd have said, "But you don't seem very happy about finishing. Do you want to tell me why?"

Here, the father is being empathetic. He's fully understanding how his son feels and is willing to listen. His son feels supported and understood, and that gives him a sense of security and the confidence to say what's on his mind. Being empathetic means you are just trying to feel what your children feel, without judging or criticizing, without saying, "You shouldn't feel that way." You simply share, listen, and understand, and only afterwards do you try to orient the child or say something to help them resolve whatever issues they are having.

To gain a sense of security and self-respect, children need to feel that others accept and understand—and don't disparage—how they feel. You can't understand your children without knowing what's going on inside their head, without climbing into their inner world. When you close the door to feeling, you are cutting off life and growth, and that causes insecurity and a lack of self-confidence in those around you. Children need to understand that you can't act on every feeling. Some feelings, however, need to be expressed and shared—so you can free yourself of them.

Three-year-old Charlotte runs to her mother. She is crying because the sound of an airplane has frightened her.

Non-empathetic response

"It's just a plane. Don't be scared." What that really means is "Don't feel what you're feeling because there's no reason to be scared of the sound of an airplane." Charlotte's mother is trying to eliminate the fear by means of a logical explanation. But sudden, loud noises often scare little kids. During times of intense emotion, logic won't help you calm your child down.

Empathetic response

"Oh my goodness" says the mother, hugging her child. "What an awful noise! I can see why it scared you." In that instant, the mother is entering her daughter's world. She accepts the child's fear. Charlotte senses that Mommy knows how she feels. She feels her mother's embrace and she feels protected and calms down. That's when logic comes into the picture.

Empathy means listening with your heart, not with your head. It's not only through words that we show that we are entering into another person's world. Tone of voice, body language and the sincerity that we convey are also very important.

Why Can't Parents Empathize with their Children?

For a mother or father to enter their children's inner world, they have to have some inner peace of their own. If your life is full of conflict or intense emotion, and you can barely handle your own problems, how can you deal with someone else's? A father of twins says, "I'm so sick and tired of all the noise at the factory and in the street that by the time I get home from work, I can barely stand to listen to my kids. All I can think about is the bills, and then on top that, I have to listen to my wife's griping. All I want to do is sleep, and I even get annoyed when I hear my kids' voices."

Ashley, whose daughter is eight years old, tells us, "I'm depressed. The fighting with my husband is constantly getting worse. I don't have the strength to go on. I feel detached from everything and everybody. All I feel like doing is locking myself in my room and crying. But I can't. I have to feed my daughter and take care of things around the house. I do everything like a robot. When my little girl asks me for something, I get irritated. Sometimes she talks to me, and I don't listen. I can't manage to just be present."

Frequently, instead of trying to understand their children, parents will argue with them or pressure them to react to situations the way they would. But children have their own way of organizing their experiences and we should respect that. Many of us are unable to tolerate differences and we insist that everyone react to things the way we do.

If you're afraid of getting in touch with your emotions, you won't be able to be empathetic. If you don't listen to the feelings of others and accept them, if you avoid talking about feelings like the plague, you won't be able to be empathetic. But if you open yourself up to your own emotions, without passing judgment, then you'll be better equipped to accept the feelings of others without judging them.

The Benefits of Empathy

Empathy is a powerful indication of sincerity. When you temporarily set aside your own point of view to be with your children, you are showing respect. You're letting them know that they're important to you. You're saying, "Your way of seeing things matters to me. Being with you in your world is worthy of my time and effort. I want to understand you because you matter to me."

This is the message you give your children every time you display empathy. It will boost their self-esteem. They'll grow up having self-confidence. They'll feel valued and, above all, they will learn to treat others this way, too. They'll be understanding of others, respectful and considerate. When children feel that their point of view is not being respected or when they feel misunderstood, their reaction is often to cut off communication. And if that happens, they grow up being strangers to their parents.

WHEN CHILDREN LACK AFFECTION

How you relate to your children will affect them for the rest of their lives. And it's important to understand that the way you relate to them *emotionally* is how they will relate emotionally to other adults when they grow up.

Jason, 28, came to our office for therapy. He said he was tired of getting into relationships with women that would last less than six months. The pattern was always the same. At first, he would be enthusiastic. He'd think, "This is the woman I've been waiting for!" But when the initial attraction was over, Jason would inevitably break it off.

Jason: "When I first met Sarah, I was convinced it would be different. But a few months into the relationship, I began to get bored. I wasn't satisfied, and it seemed like everything she did started annoying me."

Psychologist: "What did Sarah do that you found so annoying?"

Jason: "Everything. She wouldn't return my phone calls.

She talked too much when we were around other people. She was always hanging out with this friend of hers that I didn't like. For my birthday she gave me this really cheap gift. I know she loved me, but that just wasn't enough. I needed more."

At first, Jason would get really excited when he'd see her. But then, gradually, certain things she did started to bother him, and eventually, the relationship ended like all the others.

Michael, who is 32 years old, always falls in love with unattainable women.

Michael: "It's always the same story. I start relationships that, for whatever reason, have no future. Carla was married. Heather and Amanda had boyfriends they'd been with for a while and had no intention of leaving. Chloe lived in another state and was really wrapped up in her work. Ellie had just come out of a painful relationship and wasn't ready for another one. I went out with her four times and then she said we shouldn't see one another anymore."

Michael was always falling in love with a certain type of woman—distant, preoccupied with other things, and completely self-centered. He says that when he'd meet a potential romantic partner who was warm and affectionate, she wouldn't interest him. The women Michael brought into his life wanted to be the center of attention, and expected him to be accommodating and attentive to their needs. Those women wanted to be indulged. They weren't interested in a serious relationship, and they wanted more in return than what they gave. Eventually, with emotions running high, an enraged and frustrated Michael would end those relationships. Then he would sink into a deep depression until he fell in love again.

Lisa is 42 years old. She gives a lot of herself emotionally, but she's married to a man who doesn't fulfill her. He's cold and distant.

Lisa was married eleven years ago and now she has a nine-year-old daughter. She's an affectionate, nurturing mother. Her husband is an executive, who spends a lot of time at work. He comes home late, always tired and in a bad mood. Most nights when he gets home, he goes straight to his study and locks the door to work on his computer. He doesn't really participate in family life, and Lisa seldom goes out with him. She is always busy helping their daughter with her homework, or taking her to the library or ballet class. Lisa's whole life revolves around her daughter.

> Lisa: "My husband is cold as ice. Everything makes him angry. I feel very alone. He never listens to me. He's not interested in how I feel or what I'm worried about. I always hoped that someday he'd change."

All of these individuals suffer from emotional deprivation. They all feel like something is missing, and nothing fulfills them. They feel like no one cares what happens to them, no one is listening—and they are always unsatisfied. These feelings form long before they get into a relationship. It starts in early infancy, when a child feels that "no one's there for me."

During our first therapy session, Jason said, "I feel so alone, like I'm disconnected from everyone. I don't really feel close to anyone, not my family, not my friends, not even to girlfriends I've had."

Some people who suffer from emotional deprivation can be too demanding. They are insatiable, and no matter how much they are given, they're unsatisfied. Others, like Lisa, go out with people they "know" won't be able to give them what they need.

In Jason's case, Sarah had spent three days getting ready for his birthday party, and she had even made him a cake from scratch. But the only thing Jason could remember was that her gift wasn't expensive.

Michael was only attracted to women who, for whatever reason, couldn't give him what he needed. It seemed like they were either married or lived too far away. What they all had in common, though, was that they were beautiful and completely self-centered. They weren't sensitive to Michael's needs.

What causes emotional deprivation?

Usually emotional deprivation is rooted in the child's relationship with their mother. The mother figure is at the center of a child's world, and when they become adults, all of their major relationships, including romantic relationships, are modeled on this relationship.

Emotional deprivation can occur when there are a lot of kids in the family or when the mother works and gets home so tired that she has nothing else to "give." It also happens with mothers who suffer from depression, and spend a lot of time sleeping or watching television—any situation that makes the child think, "my mother is not here for me."

Emotional deprivation can occur when:

- The mother is cold, distant and unaffectionate.
- The child doesn't feel loved, valued, unique or special.
- The mother doesn't devote enough time and attention to their child.

- The mother is not attentive to her child's physical and emotional needs.
- The mother abandons her children or leaves them with other members of the family for long periods of time.

Jason suffered emotional deprivation as a child. His mother became pregnant when she was fifteen. His father was an older man who had been married before, and he never recognized his son. To get the support she needed, his mother spent much of her time looking for other men.

> Jason: "My mother was always busy. The minute she got back from work, she would start getting ready to go out again. When I asked her to spend time with me, she'd tell me to do my homework and make sure to eat right because she was really busy."

Lisa's sense of deprivation wasn't as apparent. She spent a lot of time with her mother, but instead of seeing her as an individual with her own needs, Lisa's mother saw her daughter as "an extension of herself." She wanted Lisa to do all the things she was never able to.

> Lisa: "My mother would take me shopping and dress me up like a doll. But when we'd get back home, she would ignore me completely. It's like I didn't matter anymore. I was like an object to be taken out and displayed so she could be proud."

Lisa felt that she was only there to satisfy her mother's desires. And as an adult, a pattern developed. She married a wealthy man (which was what her mother wanted) but it didn't make her happy.

Michael, who always fell in love with unavailable

women, had all the material things he needed—toys, clothes, the best schools. But there was a huge vacuum in his life. His mother was a famous TV announcer. She was completely devoted to her profession. She didn't spend a lot of time at home, but was up-to-date on the latest TV shows and all the new celebrities. She went to the gym every day and spent hours on her physical appearance. Being affectionate with her son was hard for her, although she loved him more than anything. Michael grew up without emotional nurturing from his mother. He was constantly trying to call attention to himself, but without much luck. His mother was always busy with other things. When he became an adult, Michael became demanding with women and sought affection from people who couldn't give it to him. He was trapped in the same cycle that began in his childhood.

Emotional deprivation, both in childhood and as an adult, causes a feeling that "something's missing," and those who suffer from it are never satisfied with what they have. Many people with emotional deprivation say, "I had a normal childhood. My parents gave me everything I needed."

It's not always easy to figure out if you are lacking something emotionally, even if you remember feeling lonely or needing attention when you were little. Remember to listen to your child, even if you think what they're saying is not too important. Turning off the TV, stopping what you're doing in order to look them in the eye and listen attentively will make them feel like they are important to you. Ask them how they feel about different situations, be affectionate, plan activities with them, and show them that they'll always be able to count on you.

HOW TO HELP CHILDREN OVERCOME ENVY

Envy comes from comparing ourselves to other people and coveting what we don't have. It's completely natural, and most children experience it at some point while growing up. It's important not to embarrass or ridicule children for having these feelings, and it's even more important not to punish them for it. Envy can be a positive thing, like when you admire someone and you want to emulate them. It is negative, though, when it causes us to hurt others or become resentful and bitter, and when it interferes with our social relationships. Although the words *envy* and *jealousy* are used interchangeably, jealousy often involves a third person and is usually defined as the fear of losing something you have, especially a lover. In this chapter, we'll be discussing envy—the desire for something you don't have. And with envy, there are usually only two people involved.

Being envious over an object that belongs to someone else can trigger rage. "Negative" envy doesn't appear in young children. It develops as a young person grows older, and is common in children and teenagers who experience emotional or material deprivation—when they are not content with what they have or who they are, which is a sign of low self-esteem.

Preventing Envy

Parents should notice when envy first starts to become an issue for their children. If it is allowed to grow and develop, it can become a lasting personality trait, embittering their lives, creating conflict and negatively affecting their relationships. All of us have desired something that belongs to somebody else, but if this desire becomes chronic and causes us pain rather than giving us an incentive to strive toward a goal, then envy has become an unproductive personality trait.

To fully understand how a child is feeling, it is important not only to observe their reactions but also to spend time listening to them. Many parents make the mistake of thinking that by simply talking to their children, they've established meaningful communication with them. That's usually not the case. You also have to listen. If your child is not particularly communicative, you can encourage them by asking questions. Most children don't know how to express how they feel. They don't have the vocabulary to put their emotions into words. That's why you should talk to them about how you felt in various situations when you were a child. Then ask them questions like, "How did you feel when Daddy said he couldn't get you a computer, even though your cousin Jacob has one?"

It is also important to help your children understand other peoples' feelings, with questions like, "How do you think your brother Ryan feels when you take away his bicycle? How would you feel if he did that to you?" If you can get your children to identify their emotions (such as envy) they'll be better prepared to cope with them. Make sure to set aside enough time to talk—and listen—to your children. Often, they don't speak if they think it's not important or that nobody's listening to them. Bedtime is a very good time to talk about their day. It's a time of relaxation and intimacy that lends itself well to communicating about feelings. If you discuss envy, don't judge them, or make them feel like they're bad kids, or that it's a sin. That only makes them feel guilty, and it doesn't stop the envy. Show them that their best friend may have beautiful, expensive things, but maybe they don't have a mother who listens to them or a grandmother who makes them their favorite dessert.

A good way to handle envy is by getting your child to value the things they have, without rejecting the possibility of getting what they want at some point in the future. Comparing your children to others creates envy. Avoid directly comparing siblings or cousins, things like: "Your notebook is a lot neater than your brother's." Instead, say: "I really like how neat your notebook is." Or instead of "Your sister's been a lot more helpful around the house lately," you could say, "I know you could be a lot more helpful around the house if you wanted to be."

We all need to feel unique to develop high self-esteem. Show every child that they're special, loved and valued—not just part of a group of brothers and sisters. Spend quality time with each child. Don't buy them all the same things—give each what they need. One might need a pair of shoes, but another might need a pair of pants. Providing for their individual needs will make them feel like individuals. Praise each child's best qualities, not just those that most appeal to you. One child might be very cooperative and responsible, while another is excellent at math, and a third in sports. If you give each child the attention and love that they need, they'll develop high self-esteem instead of envy. They'll believe in themselves and they'll achieve what they set out to do.

Finally, try to figure out if you're harboring envious feelings yourself. If so, you should start working on your own self-esteem. That would be the best example you could set for your children.

HOW BEING AWAY FROM PARENTS AFFECTS CHILDREN

Infants don't have the ability to protest when they're left alone with a stranger, but that doesn't stop them from resenting it deeply. From early on, small babies have an understanding of what is happening around them. They can sense when they're in a different environment, or in a different bed, or when they're not hearing the same sounds as usual. They know when a different person picks them up, when they are not hearing the same voice. But because infants have no perception of time, they don't understand that Mommy will be back later to get them, and they experience this temporary separation as the total disappearance of their mother, causing them profound anxiety. A child can manifest this painful experience by crying or getting sick. Illness in children is often a physical response to a distressing situation.

Alicia, who is 26, leaves her five-month-old daughter in daycare when she goes to work. At 9:30 every morning, her baby is in perfect health, but several times a week, the daycare center calls her at around eleven o'clock to let her know her baby has a fever. Alicia has to leave work to take her baby to the hospital, where it seems like the doctors can never figure out the cause of her daughter's illness. If Alicia takes her baby straight home, the fever sometimes disappears on its own. This is clearly a case of reacting to separation, which manifests itself in the form of a fever.

Often, children express their distress only when they return home. They cry, have trouble sleeping or lose their appetite. When that happens, the child is having a "delayed reaction" to separation anxiety. Obviously, all babies are different, but for most infants, separation becomes more difficult around six to eight months after they're born. At that age, children become more aware of their mother's absence. They begin to recognize people's faces accurately, and they sometimes cry in the presence of strangers. Often, by the time children start walking, they cry and run after their mothers when they leave. And if someone tries to stop them, they may start crying again or acting rebelliously, refusing to eat or to let anybody touch them.

If children appear calm when they are separated from their mothers, it doesn't mean they're not upset. It's possible they are just not showing their feelings directly. Their pain can manifest as "regression." That's when toilet-trained children start wetting their pants, or they want to go back to their baby bottle.

How long this crisis lasts depends on the individual child and the mother, as well as the conditions under which the separation takes place. Don't celebrate just because the child isn't showing any signs of being upset, though. It could just mean that they aren't expressing how they feel. That's a dangerous situation because it could mean the effects of this separation will only become evident later in the child's emotional development.

Martin was separated from his mother for the first time when he was three months old. He was taken to a babysitter's house while his mother was working. His mother changed babysitters three times after that, and there never seemed to be any issues with it. "He had no trouble adjusting... not at all," says his mother.

Martin is now six years old. He's very shy and doesn't interact much with his schoolmates. He doesn't respond to his teacher and, most of the time, he would rather be alone. On weekends, he plays quietly by himself, close to his mother, instead of joining in games with his cousins.

Martin didn't seem to be affected by separation anxiety when the separation took place, but these experiences affected his behavior later on. Often, screaming and yelling when they are separated from their parents is actually preferable to burying their feelings in the moment. Martin doesn't trust people because he's afraid that they'll "abandon" him. Every time he was given to a babysitter, she ended up disappearing from his life, and this happened over and over. The only person who always came back was his mother, and that's why she's the only person he trusts now.

When Children Are Left in Other Countries

Leaving some or all of their children in their country of origin is common among immigrants, who often bring them to their new country one at a time, once they become established. A lot of immigrant parents believe their children will be better off if they stay with their grandparents or aunts and uncles instead of having to adapt to such a different environment. Perhaps from the standpoint of security and stability, they are better off, but emotionally, they will always be resentful.

Even if children left behind by immigrant parents understand why their parents left, they can't help feeling abandoned. They feel that "there are more important things to my mother than me, so I must be worthless and unimportant." These feelings lower their self-esteem. If a child is very young when this happens, they won't be able to understand why their parents went so far away. Of course, if they're older, they might understand the logical explanations, but that won't stop them from feeling abandoned.

As adults, we understand that our loved ones are taken away forever when they die. We know that death is inevitable. But understanding that logically doesn't help you avoid the pain of loss. And the same thing happens to children. Understanding why they've been left behind doesn't make them feel any less abandoned. That's why when parents finally bring their children to their adopted country years later, they often end up being rebellious and full of rancor. Often, their rage isn't conscious, and children can't even express it in words. Instead they manifest their feelings through their behavior. A feeling of "you abandoned me and now you're going to pay for it" can be at the root of rebellious behavior. Some lose all interest in study or start doing things just to attract attention. Things like that definitely should not be ignored. Your child's future is at stake. Remember, it's harder for children who have been separated from their parents for a long time to adapt to their surroundings. They develop low self-esteem, insecurity, a lack of self-confidence, and a rebellious nature. And no matter what parents do, it never seems to be enough. They always want more.

It's important for parents to explain the reasons why they left. Don't give excuses, just explain the reality. Make sure to show your children love and affection, especially physical displays of affection like hugging and kissing. You are making up for lost time, and you may have to completely rebuild the mother/child or father/child relationship from scratch. If parents and children haven't shared daily life for a long time, they don't really know each other anymore. They are almost like strangers. They haven't been there for their child's first word or their first steps. They haven't taken their child to school or maybe they missed it when their daughter menstruated for the first time. Children in this situation have learned not to need their parents. They might think, "Now that you're here, I don't need you anymore." Feelings like that create a wall in parent-child communication.

Learning to share and communicate is hard when there has been a long-term separation. Parent and child alike are strangers and they have to get to know one another all over again. Sometimes mixed feelings make this even harder, especially when parents have had other children in the meantime, or if they brought some of their kids to live with them before others. The ones who stayed behind are bound to be jealous of their siblings. It is important to understand these feelings and to establish an environment of open communication in which children feel loved and understood.

WHAT TO DO ABOUT RAGE

There is so much fighting in some homes that violence is considered "normal," just a way of life. Instead of gentleness and loving care, these homes foster bitterness, pain, anger and resentment. And even when things seem calm without any apparent physical attacks, there's shouting, tormented emotions, and a lot of insults being thrown around.

You've probably read about child abuse or seen it on TV and found it repugnant and incomprehensible. But although many parents feel rage, they never get to the point of causing irreparable harm to their children. Rage often takes you by surprise. It takes over and you just snap, crossing the psychological boundaries you've constructed to contain your anger. And when it's over, you are just as frightened by your anger as your children are. You might also feel ashamed, and later, when you see your children in bed fast asleep, you ask for forgiveness as you lean forward and kiss them on the cheek.

Parents who have experienced this know the frustration

of harboring tenderness and rage—such opposite feelings—at the same time. "How could this possibly have happened?" they ask themselves while standing at their child's bed. "Why did I do that? And how could I have even felt that?" And now, on top of tenderness and rage, they feel guilty.

Rebecca is a sweet, uncomplicated woman of thirty-five. She came to therapy because of her anger toward her second daughter, seven-month-old Caroline. As she talks, she is constantly twisting a handkerchief between her fingers, and her feelings of guilt and despair are almost palpable. "I yell at Caroline almost every day, over and over… and I hit her. She's had colic ever since she was born, and we've lost a lot of sleep because of that. I can't stand hearing her cry. She'll stop when I pick her up, but as soon as I put her back into her crib, she starts again. My husband doesn't help. He just sits there and tells me to make her be quiet. Sometimes when I'm trying to cook, my other daughter, who's two, starts poking around into everything. Then she makes Caroline start crying, and I just can't stand it."

"Is that when you hit Caroline?" we ask.

"Yes."

"How often do you hit her?"

"Sometimes I shake her. Once or twice I've thrown her down in her crib, but never on the floor. And sometimes I just keep hitting her until I calm down. Later, I feel so guilty. She's so small and defenseless. I pray to God to forgive me, to help me solve this. I've gone to a few ministers who told me my demons had been expelled, but that only makes me feel better for two or three days, and then it happens all over again."

When Rebecca began therapy, we discovered that her rage began when she was still a baby. Her alcoholic father would beat her mother, and she was forced to repress the anger this caused her. Repressing her emotions caused her anger to build up, and when she's exposed to situations that trigger her, the floodgates open. Therapy has helped Rebecca control herself and stay calm. It's also helped her marital relationship—her husband has started to discipline the children. The couple has learned to set limits for their daughter and to avoid being manipulated by Caroline when she cries every time she is left in her crib.

Verbal Abuse

Parents express their anger in different ways—shouting, insults, criticism, slamming doors, and even by changing their plans, like when they cancel trips to the park.

The more they try to control their outbursts, the more violent they become, and the more they regret it later. Infidelity, stress, alcoholism and drugs can all play a role. To deal with their guilt, some parents try to rationalize their outbursts. "My kids don't listen to me. If I don't yell at them, they just do whatever they please," etc.

If your children don't obey you, find a different way to discipline them. You can do that without attacking them. Workshops and books can provide effective tools to help you set proper limits.

A father tells us, "There are days when I get up in the morning and I promise myself that not a single harsh word is going to come out of my mouth. But by noon, I'm beside myself and screaming abuse. And this happens over and over again."

Not all parents are concerned about their anger. Some tear down their children without the least bit remorse, while others suffer so much that they wish they had hurt themselves instead. A mother tells us, "I can't take how she looks at me. She looks scared and really hurt. It pains me, but I do it again anyway. I love my little girl and don't want her to be afraid of me, but I can't control myself."

Luke has learned to blow up when things don't go his way. He rips up his notebooks and smashes his toys against the wall. "He's just like his father!" his mother tells us. "When things don't go his way, he gets furious."

Anger can be caused by many different things and should be treated in therapy. Here's a list of a few different types of anger.

Misplaced Anger

This is when you target someone who is not the real cause of your anger. For example, a woman who is angry at her boss may not express it in the office, but takes it out on her husband and children when she gets home. A man who is furious with his wife might kick a door or a dog. Anger that's directed at children often has absolutely nothing to do with them.

Pent-up Anger

Usually, this type of anger is an issue for people who have a hard time expressing their feelings. They're in the habit of letting their frustration build up to the point where they can no longer control it. The most trivial incident can make them explode. Similarly, parents who have a hard time being firm with their kids alternate between letting them do whatever they want and blowing up at them.

Rage Caused by Emotional Instability

Anxiety, lack of rest, financial worries, insecurity and fear can all cause you to blow up.

If you have issues you can't resolve on your own, don't just let it go. Holding it in for a long time could result in rage that you don't know the cause of. If this happens, seek professional help. Rage is like fire—it consumes not only you, but also everyone around you.

EARLY ADOLESCENCE ISSUES

The pre-teen years are especially hard for parents because they're dealing with situations that are entirely new—both for them and their children.

Josephine, age twelve, doesn't tell her mother what she does at school anymore. Worse still, she shuts herself up in her room and stays on the phone for hours, keeping her voice low so no one overhears her. Once, when her mother went into Josephine's room to ask her to put her clothes away, she was writing something in her notebook and snapped, "You could have knocked! There's just no peace and quiet in this house."

Josephine's attitude is normal for her age. At that age, a child starts needing privacy and demanding respect. They get upset if parents walk into their rooms uninvited. They don't want their parents to touch them or go through their things, and they certainly don't want parents overhearing their conversations on the phone. It's not that they have something to hide. They just need some privacy, to separate themselves from the controlling eyes of their parents. They need to have their own experiences, which allows them to become more self-aware and to get in touch with their emotions. They don't even want their brothers and sisters "sticking their noses where they don't belong." By the age of ten or eleven, boys and girls start wanting their own room, separate from their brothers and sisters, and they no longer want to share their favorite things. This need for "individuality" should be respected. It is a part of their growth process—they are trying to "make a place for themselves" in the world. Young people feel invaded when their parents don't give them a little "space" and they're prone to react violently. "Mom, if Rachel touches my DVDs again, I'm going to hit her," warns a fourteen-year-old in reference to her younger sister.

Another major concern for parents is how their teenagers dress. Pre-teenagers no longer want their parents to make their clothing choices for them, and they don't care what their parents think about the clothes they wear.

Jimmy is going to his uncle's birthday party at an elegant, fancy restaurant. When his mother asks him what he's going to wear, he says his blue jeans and a green cotton shirt. "They'll never let you in dressed like that!" his mother shouts, horrified at the suggestion. "You have a perfectly nice navy blue suit, and I'll buy you a new tie to go with it." "I'll wear whatever I please," Jacob responds, "and if they don't like it, I'm staying home."

Many mothers complain that their daughters wear the same clothes all week long without washing them, or that they can't stand seeing them wear short skirts and tacky jewelry. "Sometimes when she leaves the house she looks like she's in a disguise!" one mother tells us. But keep in mind is that the over-the-top clothing and jewelry are covering up a lot of anxiety. And they are much more concerned with how they look to their friends than to their parents.

The more insecure a young person is, the more they try to cover up that insecurity with loud clothing that conforms to their friends' tastes. They need to feel accepted by the group, and the more they fear not being accepted for what's inside, the more they need to be flashy on the outside. Many young people go shopping with a friend to get the opinion of a person of their own age.

I Can't Look like Mom and Dad!

Teenagers almost never want to be in their parents' presence. This is particularly true in early adolescence. They don't want to look like their parents and they need to convince everyone they're doing things their own way. They are trying to establish an identity of their own, so they completely reject their parents as role models. Since they are seeking role models outside of the home, they often imitate friends or classmates, and they have a great deal of admiration for their favorite actors, singers or sports figures. They think these role models are "awesome" and "perfect," and they want to be just like them. That's why they want to dress like a pop singer or wear their hair like their favorite movie star. At the same time, they need to be accepted and feel like they "belong to a group." That's why you can see so many dressed alike, with the same hair style.

Mona, whose daughter is 14 years old, complains, "Now Catherine wants a pair of boots exactly like the ones her best friend wears, and last week they both bought the same leather jacket. They look ridiculous going around dressed exactly alike. It's like my daughter has no personality of her own!" This is a common complaint among parents with teenagers. However, it's just a phase, and they'll outgrow it as soon as they start discovering their own likes and dislikes. Many parents feel hurt when their adolescent rejects anything and everything that they suggest. But usually, teenagers aren't trying to hurt their parents on purpose. And it's not that their children don't love them—they just need to find their own place in the world. We've all done that at some point. It is an important step toward reaching maturity.

Remember, it's a phase that will pass, and to understand it, you'll need to look at both what's going on inside your child's head as well as the changes taking place in the outside world. Our society has a profound influence on youth, and when they reach adolescence, they begin to look beyond the family circle to figure out their values, their ideas about fashion, and how they want to act. When parents try to "force" their kids to ignore outside influences, much like their parents and grandparents probably did, the only thing they accomplish is to alienate their children, and that can cause a breakdown in communication.

It's really hard for parents to always keep a close eye on the changes their adolescent is going through, but it is absolutely necessary to make an effort. You simply can't expect them to live and think like an adult. "Climb down" from your lofty parental perspective and try to understand this stage in your adolescent's life—sometimes they are still children, but sometimes they're adults. They might pretend to know things they don't know, but they need to be supported and protected. That requires patience, understanding and "a big heart." Don't be too quick to judge your adolescent. Be there for them when they need help. Often it's about being a "silent companion," quietly letting them know that you can be counted on when they need you. Other times, you'll need to be strict, setting limits to prevent disaster. And above all, learn not only to talk, but to listen as well. When pre-teens feel they're not being listened to, they distance themselves.

The parent-child relationship goes through some profound changes when adolescence begins, yet many parents have the same attitude that they had when their child was younger, and that makes adolescents resentful and upset. They react angrily and start to rebel. Remember, balance is key.

Strict or Soft?

Parents who have the hardest time are the ones who are too rigid, who refuse to put up with the contradictions that adolescence brings. By being too strict, these parents lose control over their children, who start hiding things. But parents who are too soft also end up losing control because their adolescent doesn't have any limits. When there is no supervision, they may feel unloved, that no one cares about what happens to them. Ideally there is a middle ground—as your child demonstrates greater responsibility, give them some more leeway, but make sure any new limits you set are clear. For instance, if your teenager has come home on time all year long, try setting their new curfew one hour later. Of course, parents set limits according to their individual religious, moral and cultural values, but within that framework, the limits should never be either too strict or too lax.

CONSEQUENCES OF A PAINFUL EXPERIENCE

Unexpected or painful experiences leave us with powerful memories. If these memories don't go away within a few days, and you continue to be haunted by images, or if you feel emotionally numbed, you could be suffering from post-traumatic stress disorder (PTSD). Trauma is an emotional shock to the system. When it has been particularly powerful, unexpected or sudden, you may never be able to be the same person you once were. Symptoms may emerge that affect your ability to function as an individual or in relationships.

PTSD has been studied extensively among combat veterans, who have had to live through especially powerful experiences and emotional "blows." Their trauma is manifested through behavioral changes.

But PTSD can occur at any age and in many different situations, like accidents, the death of a loved one, being suddenly abandoned by a partner, losing a job, witnessing intense situations such as the death, being raped or otherwise physically abused.

Symptoms of PTSD include:

- Nightmares about the traumatic event.
- Flashbacks.
- Excessive sensitivity to situations similar to the traumatic event (for example, if the anniversary of 9/11, or the days immediately afterwards) triggers intense anxiety and causes you to relive that traumatic incident.
- Avoidance of emotions associated with the trauma. For example, forty-year-old Cathy couldn't stand seeing car accidents on television because of the one she had been in five years earlier.
- Some people have partial loss of memory with regard to events connected with the trauma. For instance, one young woman who was gang-raped couldn't recall whether it was three or four men who assaulted her, and she wasn't able to remember their faces. However, she was able to remember their voices.
- In young children, the loss of skills that they have already learned, like going to the bathroom on their own or speaking—in other words, regression to earlier stages of development.
- A feeling of disconnection or separation from others; feeling alone even when sitting in a room surrounded by family and friends.
- Inability to love or trust other people.
- Frequently, loss of any hope for the future, for example, marriage, professional or financial success.
- Trouble getting to sleep at night, or a tendency to wake up repeatedly during the night.
- Difficulty concentrating.
- Loss of contact with reality or disconnecting for

seconds or minutes while reliving images of the traumatic event.

- Reliving the traumatic event over and over. This can make it dangerous for a PTSD victim to drive a car or be responsible for small children.
- Overreacting to situations that remind the victim of the trauma. For example, after one young woman was assaulted and robbed in an elevator, her hands would start to sweat and her heart would race every time she got into one.

Numbness

This is one of the most common symptoms of PTSD. During one of her therapy sessions, 32-year-old Tanya told us:

Tanya: "When I was 19 years old, I was raped. For a long time, I would only talk about it intellectually, as if it had happened to someone else. I mean, I knew it had happened to me, but I didn't feel anything. I had trouble having intimate relations with men. For some reason, the relationship would always end before I got to the point of intimacy. I was raped on New Year's Day. For years, whenever the holiday season approached, I'd start feeling anxious. I didn't want to participate in any New Year's celebrations ever again. I felt disconnected from my family. I wanted to sleep through the holiday season and only wake up when it was next year. I finally realized how bad off I was when I met a man who wanted a serious relationship. I realized that even though I liked him a lot, I wasn't going to be able to have a sexual relationship with him. When he began to pressure me, I wanted to end the relationship, but at the same time I felt tremendously distraught and began to cry all the time. I couldn't move on and I couldn't escape. I felt trapped. He suggested I get help, and that's what made me decide to come to therapy. I really want to overcome this situation and be able to be happy with a man."

This is a typical case of someone who thinks she has overcome the trauma. Tanya can talk about it calmly, but in her daily life, she finds herself "limited and trapped," especially when faced with situations that remind her of the traumatic event or when the anniversary of the trauma draws near.

Children also suffer this kind of stress following a traumatic experience. They may manifest PTSD through lack of concentration, changes in behavior, withdrawal, hypersensitivity, or insomnia. If a child exhibits any of these symptoms, have them undergo a psychological evaluation to figure what might have happened. Because of fear or shame, children may not readily express their trauma, even if they are deeply affected by it. Trauma may leave its mark in a number of areas and keeps children from developing their skills or achieving success. Unresolved trauma can keep people from enjoying their life, even when they seem to have everything they need.

If PTSD symptoms last more than three months after the traumatic event, seek the advice of a therapist. Otherwise, the symptoms could become chronic, and that can lead to depression, extreme anxiety, or drug and alcohol abuse. If treated, symptoms usually disappear within 2 months.

HOW CHILDREN DEFEND THEMSELVES

Every child needs approval from adults. And when you don't acknowledge their efforts to improve themselves and to develop their skills, they usually don't have a problem pointing it out for you.

"Hey Dad! Look how strong I am!"

"Look, I can go downstairs without holding the rails."

"Look Mommy, I finished eating before Emily!"

"Watch me write my name!"

Are they just boasting? No. To create a positive image of themselves, they need positive reinforcement and acknowledgement from adults. How parents respond to them throughout this process is key. If children don't get the recognition that they need, they won't respect themselves and when that happens, one of three things can occur:

1. They develop ways of hiding their perceived inadequacy.
2. They withdraw from reality and begin fantasizing as a way of counteracting their sense of rejection.

3. They accept their inadequacy, and begin a life of self-defeating behaviors.

Most kids will experiment with all sorts of defense mechanisms before withdrawing into their fantasy world. Usually that's their last resort. But each of these three paths comes with its own price.

The "Cover Up"

Building defenses by covering up inadequacies is a weapon against fear, anxiety, or a sense of failure.

Anita often bad-mouths her siblings while exaggerating her own accomplishments. When she sees one of her brothers doing something wrong, she runs straight to her parents to let them know. She always tries to convince her parents that they're not "good boys," while highlighting her own good behavior.

Joshua likes to show that he's the strongest and sometimes he manages to impose his will on other kids.

Carrie talks non-stop, and doesn't let anyone get a word in edgewise. It's her way of drawing attention to herself.

These are examples of defense mechanisms that come from low self-esteem, a feeling of being bad and unworthy of being loved. These three children are covering up their lack of self-worth. The more effort they make to be noticed, the more they show that they believe that no one will value them if they don't. Parents should ask themselves what they could have done to give their kids that idea. This "secret" feeling of low self-esteem is at the root of their neurotic behavior.

Neurosis is just a scar that forms around a psychological wound. A child who has a strong sense of self-worth won't build defenses.

Eight-year-old Marissa is loud, bossy and domineering.

But scolding or punishing her won't help—she is covering up feelings of being useless and clumsy. If her parents want to help, first they need to find out what it is that she is hiding.

One solution for Marissa would be to get some training in a sport that she likes. That would show, in a positive way, that she isn't at all useless or clumsy. She'll start convincing herself and others of her strengths and abilities, and that will raise her self-esteem. She'll no longer need to "cover up" her feelings of worthlessness with an exaggerated sense of self.

Not all children (or adults) find constructive ways of improving their self-esteem, and many choose to create more defense mechanisms that only lead them to self-destructive behaviors.

Imagine that Marissa doesn't find her solution in sports and continues being loud, bossy and domineering. This will make her feel left-out and rejected by others, which will lead to even lower self-esteem. As her relationships continue to deteriorate, she'll be less and less able to concentrate on her studies. Feeling accepted by her peers will become more important than learning her multiplication tables. Later on, this could lead to attention-seeking behavior like wearing tasteless clothing or going out with a lot of guys or even joining a gang.

Everything Seems Just Fine

Some teenagers with feelings of inadequacy put on a happy face as their defense. Brianna's parents only appreciated her when she was nice and when she did her homework. As long as she played the "little angel" she got all the affection and recognition she needed. So Brianna learned to hide her feelings of rage, frustration, jealousy and anxiety. On the surface, everything seemed to be just fine. She took care to maintain her "good girl" image to get affection from her family. She was constantly seeking the approval of others, and made a lot of effort to cover up anything "bad." She devoted more energy to how she was perceived than to really being a good person. This kept her from realizing her potential and her self-esteem suffered. Brianna ended up being an unsatisfied adult, who was out of touch with her feelings and constantly pretending to be someone she wasn't.

Some people don't want others to see their true Ego, because they consider themselves unacceptable, but constructing a false Ego always ends in failure. People react to a "mask," not the real person, and the true Ego doesn't get a chance to express itself or to communicate with others.

Susan was born into a family that liked to throw parties, and she learned to get recognition from her family by being "the life of the party." She always knew how to put on a happy face, but the loneliness behind the mask sapped so much of her energy that by the time she reached adulthood, she would spend much of her time in bed, always with some sort of illness. She began psychotherapy at the age of forty-five, and it helped her learn to accept her true, calm, meditative nature. She came to the realization that she had lived her life acting, in order to win affection. Therapy helped her to live in accordance with her true self. Many of her friends and family members appreciated the change, and she learned that she could get affection simply by being herself.

The woman who doesn't want anyone to see her without makeup, or the person who gets desperate when someone knocks on the door when the house is a mess will do almost anything to keep others from catching a glimpse of "their reality." They give too much importance to the exterior while trying to hide what's on the inside, which to their mind, isn't "good." Masks are used to cover up a "worthless" Ego.

Many people believe that in order to be loved, they have to appear to be "good," efficient, competent, perfect, and they put a lot of effort into constructing beautiful masks. What they don't realize is that they're actually just fooling themselves.

Re-examining old habits that you carry with you from childhood helps you realize that you don't need your old masks, and that you will be loved regardless. Authenticity is captivating.

Submission

Children who can't manage to create adequate defenses will submit.

Barbara didn't get a lot of recognition from her parents. Just about everything she did or said was wrong. She had a domineering father who shouted a lot and had a disdainful attitude toward women. Throughout her childhood, Barbara saw her mother playing the role of a doormat. She grew up thinking that she didn't deserve the least bit of respect or consideration. As an adult, she always attracted men who treated her badly and constantly reminded her of how worthless she was. She was stuck in this situation until she decided to begin therapy. Through therapy, Barbara managed to raise her self-esteem and break out of this "pattern" that dominated her life.

CURIOSITY AND CHILDREN

Human beings are naturally curious, and children are especially so. They interact with the things around them without letting pre-established ideas about them interfere with their perceptions of "how things should be." When you support and stimulate a child's curiosity, it gives them a "ticket" to learn. Whether or not a child learns easily depends on their parents' attitude about curiosity.

At about age three or four, a child will start to ask "Why?" *"Why is the sky blue? Why does fire burn? Why is the moon sometimes full and sometimes not? Does God have eyes? Why are you putting on those shoes?"*

At about age five, their *attitude* towards learning has been established, and this attitude has a lot to do with how their parents have reacted to their questions and explorations.

Unfortunately, by the age of five, many children have also learned not to learn. Alexander takes his big-wheeled toy truck and turns it over on its back. His mother says, *"Alexander, cars don't go like that,"* and she reaches out and flips it over for him. *"Alexander, don't make noise with your spoon,"* she says, and grabs the spoon out of his hand. Time and again, his mother stops Alexander from investigating and exploring, from seeing how the wheels go around on his truck when it's turned over, from hearing how the spoon sounds when he bangs it against his fork. His mother doesn't allow him to try out new ideas. Alexander starts to think that every time he tries something new he's going to be scolded, "corrected" or even punished. The child quickly learns to bottle up his curiosity in order to avoid the disapproval of his parents. Clearly, there are times when experimentation is dangerous for children. But when it's not, you should allow your kids to explore and test every possibility, no matter how absurd it might seem. There's no harm in letting Alexander experiment with an upside-down truck.

Often, parents get annoyed by all the repetitive questioning. *"Go play outside. Be quiet, you're bothering me. Don't interrupt when* I'm *watching my favorite soap opera. Let me tie your shoes for you, I'm faster. Here, I'll wash your hands for you. You're too slow and you get your sleeves all wet."* If you don't give your kids a chance to explore, to get wet, to tie a knot in their shoelaces, then they'll never learn to do anything on their own. And besides, they get the message that *"You can't do this. You don't know how."* This message hurts their self-confidence and makes them think that they are, indeed, useless. But if children only get approval from their parents when they're quiet and passive, they learn to put aside their questions and their curiosity. They'd rather not make the effort and they won't want to try anything new.

It is up to parents to support their child's desire to learn. Every child needs to know that asking questions and experimenting is worthwhile, and they shouldn't feel inferior because they thirst for knowledge, or because of the mistakes they make. Childhood is for exploring, curiosity and originality.

HOW TO PREPARE CHILDREN FOR READING

A lot of children have trouble learning to read, and it's not because they lack the intelligence. They just haven't gone through all the steps. It's like building a house—if the foundation isn't sound, the building will crumble—and the same is true of reading. The proper preparation begins during pre-school. You should start providing them with reading activities when they are two or three, so that by the time they reach first grade, they will be "ready" to learn.

WHAT TO DO BEFORE YOUR CHILDREN START THE FIRST GRADE:

Teach your children to listen to and follow instructions.

You should begin doing this when your child is about a year old. Start with simple things like: "Come over here and hand me that spoon." As the child gets older, start giving more complex instructions: "Tie your shoelaces the way I showed you," "Put your jacket on before you go outside," or "Wash your hands before dinner."

Your children learn listening skills when you listen to them, so set aside some time just for listening to what they have to say. If you don't stop cooking or watching TV when they talk to you, they're going to feel a bit neglected. Stop what you're doing, get close to your child and look them in the eye when they speak. Remember, children learn by example—they'll emulate what you do.

Encourage your children to use complete sentences

Kids tend to respond to questions with one-word answers: yes, no, that, gimme, etc. It is important for children to learn to use complete sentences like, "Yes, I want to go to the grocery store with you," or "I want to keep playing." Although they can't form complete sentences when they first begin to speak, they are perfectly capable of doing so by the time they're three or four years old. It is also important for parents to use complete sentences when they speak to their kids. For instance, instead of saying, "Don't touch," say "Don't touch that vase. You might break it." Children get accustomed to hearing a sequence of words in complete sentences, and without even trying, they begin to learn grammar. You are also helping them expand their vocabulary.

Read stories to your children

If children hear their parents reading to them out loud, they'll start to think of reading as a pleasurable activity, even before they can read themselves. When they watch a lot of TV, on the other hand, they get used to the visual stimulation and lose their ability to imagine things on their own. When you read to them, they picture characters and situations in their head, and that helps them develop creativity. But when they watch too much TV, they get used to seeing images created by someone else. They *absorb*, but they don't *create*.

A good time to read a story to your children is at bedtime. Make it a daily habit that your children really enjoy. If you can get them to be enthusiastic about the stories you read to them, it will give them a great incentive to learn to read as soon as they can.

Ask your children to relate stories about what they've done and how they feel

If your child goes somewhere with one of his parents, have the other parent ask them some questions about the trip. For example, "Did you have fun at the park?" "Were there lots of other kids?" "Were you scared when it started to thunder?" Questions like these encourage them to talk, to tell their story. And, more importantly, getting them to tell you how they feel will help them get in touch with their emotions. Questions facilitate communication, and they show your children that you're interested in what they do and how they feel. Above all, good communication will kindle your child's interest in reading about others. If they see people being interested in what happens to them, they'll be interested in what happens to other people, too. It will stimulate them to open their minds and it will encourage their willingness to read and to seek knowledge.

Encourage your children to observe their surroundings and describe what they see

Try making a game out of getting your children to tell you what they see around them, particularly when you go somewhere new. This will increase their vocabulary and their powers of observation. Ask your kids to observe the differences and the similarities between the new place and places that they are already familiar with. For example, "Do you think this red sign is bigger than the one on the corner by our house?" or "Do you think this park has as many trees as the one we went to last Sunday?" Things like that help a child's mind grow accustomed to observation, comparisons, and differentiating size, color, quantity, etc.

Teach your children new words

Describing new objects and situations helps children increase their vocabulary. Parents should also correct children when they don't use a word properly. Be gentle about it, though, and don't get angry. It also doesn't help them learn to speak properly when you "baby talk." When a new word comes up, explain its meaning and provide some familiar examples. If a child asks, "What does 'fake' mean?" a good answer might be, "Remember that story about the pirate with the wooden leg? Well, that leg isn't real, but it works like a real one. That's a fake leg." Another possibility is, "When you dressed up like a clown and you put on that big red nose, that wasn't your *real* nose, it was a fake one." Using simple examples is the best way to explain new words. These examples should be concrete situations that the child has experienced—at seven or eight years of age, a child's brain isn't prepared to deal with abstract thought. New words are fun for children, and you should ask them to come up with other examples.

Objects that are the same and objects that are different

Learning to compare and contrast is crucial to your child's ability to read. Later, your child will have to learn the difference between sounds and letters. That's why it's important to develop the ability to differentiate things by the time they reach first grade. Use everyday situations as an opportunity to stimulate them and observe the differences between various shapes and objects. For instance, "Give the smaller glass to your little brother," or "Pass me that green plate, please."

A visit to the grocery store is an excellent opportunity to study differences and similarities. "Pick out tomatoes that are the same size," or "I need four potatoes—two large ones and two small ones," or "Pick out two nice, soft pears." Try to make it fun, rather than pressuring or judging your child. As always the goal is for them to develop a pleasure for learning.

Teach your children to connect different ideas

Making connections is a very important reading skill, and it's a mental function that develops early on. Infants are able to associate the sound of the refrigerator door with mealtime. A one-year-old connects Mother changing her outfit with going out. The ability to make connections improves as kids get older. You can help develop this skill by asking them questions like "Your little brother's crying. What do you think the problem is?" or "Your father didn't go to work today. What day of the week is it?"

Show your children images and have them describe what they see

When you read your children a story, make sure you look at the pictures, too, and say things like, "Look at this bird on the roof! What else do you see on the roof?" or "What is this little girl doing with her grandma?" Describing a picture is a good way to increase your child's vocabulary, and it can improve their powers of observation and association. It also motivates them to read.

Read in front of your children and be enthusiastic about it

If children never see anybody reading at home, they'll think it's not important. Develop good reading habits of your own. Find something you like, whether it's newspapers, magazines, or books—and read. How can you convey the message that reading is important if your child never sees you doing it? And mention to them how entertaining and exciting it is to read. Let them know that learning to read is not only important, but also fun. Make your children feel like it's fun to read about new things together, and let them know that once they learn how to read on their own, they'll start learning all sorts of things, and then they'll be able to share them with you. Remember that what you consider important is what they'll consider important.

Make your children feel like they're valuable and capable of learning

Your attitude towards reading is very important. Try not to be impatient. Be positive and show them that it makes you happy when they learn something new. Congratulate them, hug them, and be pleased. Satisfying their parents with their achievements is very important to children of all ages. If you lose your patience and say, "I've said this word to you a thousand times and you still don't get it," your child is going to feel stupid and incapable of learning. This will undermine their efforts to read. Keep in mind that learning is a process, and making mistakes is only natural. Learning should be a pleasant, anxiety-free experience, so don't yell or pressure them. And make sure not to take out your frustrations on them while they are reading. If your children associate learning with communication and fun, they'll be eager to learn. But if they associate it with yelling, frustration and failure, they'll avoid it.

HOW TO FIGHT JEALOUSY

No matter how much parents try to convey the idea that jealousy is wrong, most children can't help feeling jealous of others. And children who are jealous tend to feel increasingly guilty and undervalued.

What Jealousy Tells Us

What makes you jealous? Is it when people are more skilled at something? When they are more self-confident, have more success, a higher social status?

In any case, the specific reason for the jealousy isn't really what's important. What is important is that jealousy occurs when you feel you are at a disadvantage. People who are self-confident and successful usually aren't jealous of others. Simply put, the purpose of jealousy is to cover up feelings of failure.

Feeling jealous toward loved ones includes: "I feel left out," "I don't want to share you because I'm afraid of losing you," or "I'm afraid you might find someone better." But regardless of whether the disadvantage is real or imagined, the jealousy *is* real for the person who feels it.

What Makes Children Jealous?

Children yearn for their parents' love and undivided attention. Anthony watches his mother spend hours tending to the needs of his newborn brother. He wants his mother's attention and is trying to find ways of getting it. He starts having stomachaches and waking up in the middle of the night. He has also regressed to wetting his bed. He even wants to go back to his baby bottle.

Samantha noticed that her brother gets better grades than she does, even though he spends less than an hour on his homework, and then starts watching TV. She has started ripping up his notebooks.

Children who feel that they are at a disadvantage compensate by trying to make rival siblings look bad in front of their parents. And if that doesn't work, they might turn to more drastic measures, like Samantha.

So why doesn't Samantha just try to be her brother's equal? Well, it's clear that she doesn't believe she can. She lacks self-worth, and believes, "I'm not capable." Try saying things to boost her self-confidence. Pay attention to where her difficulties lie, and seek professional help if necessary. It definitely doesn't help if you say, "Don't ever tear up your brother's notebook again!" That will either make her keep doing it or find another way to express her anger, jealousy and dissatisfaction with herself.

Children who have Self-respect are less Jealous

It's important to work with each child individually to develop their unique talents and interests. Sometimes, for the sake of convenience, or to give equal treatment to their children, parents send all of their kids to karate class, or buy them all shoes at the same time. But maybe not all of them like karate and maybe some of them need a pair of pants or a blouse instead of shoes. Try to find out what each of them needs and treat them in a way that makes them feel special and unique.

It is also important to devote some time to each individual child, even if it means spending just a few minutes with them before they go to bed or letting them go with Mother, one at a time, to the grocery store. The point is to make your child feel like they're more than just "one of the herd." Make each of your children feel special. Parents rarely feel exactly the same way about all of their children. Sometimes a child has a more affinity for one parent or the other. However, when you repeatedly show favoritism to one of your children, it sets the stage for jealousy.

If you favor one of your children over the others, look inward to figure out why. Is there something about your other child that displeases you? (If so, remember that the things we don't like about other people are usually same the things we dislike about ourselves). Or perhaps the child reminds you of your own mother or father. When there's jealousy, you should examine the family situation as a whole and see if maybe you're showing favoritism to one of your children. For instance, many mothers make their oldest daughter "Mother's little helper." If that's the case, your daughter may feel she is being singled out, and that it's not fair that she has so many responsibilities that her siblings don't.

Comparing your children to each other is a surefire way to create jealousy. "Why can't you study like your sister?" Words like these make your child feel inferior and that doesn't motivate them to improve. How would you feel if your boss said, "Why can't you do your reports like Jeff? He always manages to do everything just the way we like it." You probably aren't going to like Jeff too much after that, and on top of that, you probably won't miss the chance to make him look bad if you can.

How to Combat Jealousy

One way to reduce negative feelings like jealousy is to encourage their expression—in words, drawings, paintings, music, arts and crafts, etc. Encouraging your child to express their jealousy means talking about it, and for that to happen, your child needs to feel understood. Statements like, "You shouldn't be jealous of your sister," are not helpful. Feelings don't go away when you apply logic to them, or when you order them to disappear. They have to be expressed verbally to someone who understands—not someone who is going to invalidate them.

"You love Jesse more than me!" cries Thomas. "That's the most ridiculous thing I've ever heard!" his father exclaims. "Don't I take you to play ball every Saturday? Didn't we buy you that bike you wanted for Christmas? And what about all those expensive field trips? We barely spend any money on Jesse because he's still too young to do those things, so stop whining!"

Thomas's father has just bombarded his son with "evidence" showing that there is no logical reason for him to be jealous of his little brother—and that he shouldn't be feeling what he's feeling. But jealousy is not always logical, and just by accepting its existence, you will help your children free themselves of it.

What would be a more constructive way for Thomas's father to approach his son's feeling of jealousy?

"You do more for Jesse than for me," Thomas complains.

"It seems like you're feeling neglected and left out," says Thomas's father, trying to understand what his son is feeling.

"You always hold him on your lap and read those stupid baby stories," says Thomas.

"Sounds like you don't want us to read to him," his

father responds.

"Why would I," cries Thomas. "He gets special attention just because he's younger."

Although it seems like it would make sense at this point to tell Thomas that he got this same treatment when he was Jesse's age, this type of logical answer actually won't help.

A better answer is "How would you like it if we started spending some time together at night, just you and me? We'll put Jesse to bed and then you and I can play checkers or something for half an hour before you go to bed."

Understanding his child and taking action shows that Thomas's father is also willing to give his oldest boy some special attention. That allows Thomas to set aside his jealousy, which was caused by his perception that his father paid more attention to his little brother. Thomas's father was able to get to the root of the problem and solve it. That night, Thomas slept well. He stopped thinking that his parents were paying more attention to Jesse.

Signs of Jealousy

Children seldom express themselves directly, for example, "I'm jealous of my brother," or "I don't want to share with you," or "I feel left out." Jealousy is often expressed through actions. Wetting their pants, sucking their thumb, or other child-like behavior could be a sign.

Another sign is when kids start being demanding. Jealous children may start demanding that you buy them more toys or more clothes, or that you spend more time with them. Some children try drawing attention to themselves by turning up the volume on the TV whenever Mother helps their brother or sister with their homework. Others start clowning around or breaking things intentionally. And still others may get sick frequently or start being fussy.

Pay attention to these signs, and try to get to the root of the problem instead of punishing your child. That will only cause them to repress their feelings, and they may express their jealousy in another way. Remember that children who show signs of jealousy are suffering, and anyone who has ever been jealous knows the pain, frustration and anger it can cause.

FIGHTING AMONG SIBLINGS

All parents want their children to get along with each another, but sometimes they pressure them so much that just the opposite happens.

Linda, mother of three, says, "My eight-year old constantly tells his little brother that he's an idiot. He makes him feel like he's clumsy and never does anything right. Meanwhile, my six-year-old is always bothering his big brother, intentionally breaking his things and blaming it on him."

It's clear that the older brother has a jealousy issue, which he manifests by criticizing his brother, and the younger brother gets even by intentionally doing things that he knows will upset his big brother. When their parents show up to ask who started it, they blame each other, bending reality to look "innocent." In situations like these, parents should not try to figure out which one is "guilty"—it takes two to tango.

Parents shouldn't take either child's side. It is best to work with each of them separately. If the older brother is showing signs of jealousy, show him in small ways the importance of being the oldest. Give him certain privileges for being older, and try not to "blame" him. Try saying something like, "How would you feel if someone went around telling you what an idiot you were all the time? That hurts your brother's feelings. I know you love him a lot and you really don't want to hurt him." Allow him to express his negative feelings toward his brother. Don't respond with things like, "You shouldn't say that. It's not right. That's no way to act." That will make him think, "I'm always the bad one. It's always my fault." And these thoughts will just reinforce his bad behavior. Encourage positive feelings and try to overlook the negative ones. Your child will give more energy to the things you pay attention to, and the negative stuff will gradually lose its effect if you ignore it.

Meanwhile, show your younger child that he's not dumb like his brother says. Praise him when he does a good job. Give him confidence by telling him you believe in his abilities. And let him express his feelings toward his older brother, even if they're negative. Expressing feelings releases them and makes them lose their strength. Repressed feelings, on the other hand, are just put away and buried. They become a "time bomb" that can explode out of control. Negative feelings in children are usually just a phase. If these feelings are channeled into something constructive, they will usually go away on their own. If a child says, "I hate Michael! He's always takes my toys!" it's not really hatred, but a way of expressing anger, pain and feeling powerless. This is something temporary, and it is best for it to be expressed out loud, so that it doesn't build up inside.

It is best not to intervene in clashes between siblings. If your children ask you to mediate, you can say something like, "I wasn't in the room when you started fighting, so you'll just have to work this out on your own. But you should know—there's a rule in this family, and no matter how angry you are, we never hit one another." If your children disobey rules like this, both children should be punished, but instead of shouting or hitting them, cancel their weekend trip, or take away their TV privileges, or send them to their room without dinner that evening.

Words Hurt

"In this family we never hit each other." This non-aggression pact should also include verbal abuse. Children know exactly what to say to wound their siblings. Don't let your children hurt their brother or sister's self-esteem by belittling them.

Also, if you're going to make this rule with your children, do it with your partner, too. You can't expect your children not to say hurtful words if you and your spouse do it. Remember, children learn by example, not by "doing as you say and not as you do." Parents need to be role models, and kids need to see their parents resolving their issues by talking things over, not by shouting or attacking one another verbally or physically. But problems aren't solved by keeping quiet, either. When problems go unresolved, they're bound to "explode" sooner or later.

Issues that can arise among siblings are, in fact, valuable opportunities for children to learn how to resolve their disagreements. They are practicing conflict resolution for when they become adults. You can help by giving your children incentives to express their feelings. For instance, ask "How are you feeling? I know you're upset with your brother, but try and understand why he doesn't want to lend you his model airplane. Remember how you broke his two other airplanes? He's just doesn't want you to do the same thing with this one. Talk to him, and maybe you can convince him that you'll be really careful this time." But don't intervene further. Encourage your children to handle their own problems and express themselves.

What to Do

- Encourage your children to find their own solutions.
- Don't take sides. It will make the other child feel less loved and their resentment will turn into rebelliousness later.
- Don't be a referee. They'll never learn to resolve conflict on their own.
- Don't let your children get to the point of physical or verbal abuse. If that happens, you should intervene. Demand that they respect each other. Physical fighting does nothing to help them learn to talk out their problems.
- Setting a good example is a much more powerful tool than telling them what's right and wrong.
- Encourage your children to express their feelings and communicate.

BULLYING AND SELF-DEFENSE

Young children make fun of other kids and call them names all the time. It's usually just a form of play, but it can be deeply painful. It's an everyday occurrence—a child who wears glasses is called "four-eyes," an overweight child is called "fatso," and a neat, studious child gets called "nerd."

A little bit of fooling around or the occasional name-calling is no big deal. It's a way for kids to hone their verbal skills and release their aggression—it's just friendly competition. In other words, making fun of other kids is a form of normal social exchange that occurs between individuals of the same age. It also sets boundaries for who belongs to a certain group and who doesn't. It becomes a problem, though, when this hurts other people, when the victim is not yet prepared to understand the taunting philosophically and with a sense of humor.

Many children who are made fun of develop low self-esteem and feel rejected by their peers. In some cases, children refuse to go to school—they either invent stomachaches or actually get sick in order to avoid painful situations. This can affect their performance at school and even their future relationships. If children's self-image deteriorates and they begin to feel ashamed of themselves, they won't be able to express themselves freely or develop their skills and talents.

Who Gets Made Fun Of?

Certain kids seem to be a magnet for it. These children are extremely impressionable—when they are made fun of, they react by crying, hiding or furiously chasing their "bully" to the point of breaking down.

Sometimes kids become vicious for no apparent reason. But children who are made fun of repeatedly often end up having difficulty socializing with other children their age. Why do certain children react so badly? Parents should reflect on their child's personality as well as their relationship with their child. Maybe they are not emotionally mature for their age or maybe they are being overprotected. Emotionally immature children are unprepared to adequately relate to other children their age—they don't know how to defend themselves. If that's the case, therapy can help your child catch up with other kids their age.

Children with low self-esteem, who don't value themselves, or who often feel ashamed of themselves subconsciously attract taunting. Children are highly perceptive. They know right away who they'll get a reaction out of. If they try it once and it works, they'll do it again, seeking the same reaction. Children tend to form cliques, and often when one starts making fun of somebody, others will join in, further aggravating the situation for the victim.

What Can Parents Do?

First and foremost, children who have been bullied by

other kids need their parents to comfort and understand them. Allow them to express how they feel, their anger and their pain. Don't tell them that it doesn't matter, because to them it certainly does. Parents should not say "don't pay any attention" to the other kids or "just ignore them" because that, unfortunately, does not work. Bullies often grow even more vicious when their victims are silent. Kids need to learn to live with others, and that means figuring out how to respond to unpleasantness.

It's important to teach your children how to "roll with the punches" and return them. It's not about learning martial arts or always turning the other cheek. It's a question of developing effective defense strategies.

First of all, a physical response should be avoided. Explain to your children that violence never solves anything. Practice at home, and build trust. For instance, try making a game out of coming up with nicknames for family members. This can help children learn how to come up with witty responses, and they'll realize that being made fun of isn't the end of the world. Also, games like these teach them to exercise their creativity and increase their vocabulary.

Also, encourage your children to develop skills that can compensate for their "flaws." For instance, if your children have "ears like Dumbo" or they're a few pounds overweight, they can get respect by learning how to tell jokes, or doing magic tricks, or playing basketball like a pro. They'll not only keep their self-esteem high, but also start feeling proud of themselves.

Parents as defenders?

A common mistake is for parents to take on the role of guardian angel or defense attorney for their children. Naturally, you don't want to see your kids suffer, but you won't be doing them any favors if you get involved in a conflict among peers. Children have to learn to fend for themselves so that in the future they'll be armed with the tools they need to handle tough situations. However, if the situation has gone beyond simple fun—if, for example, your child is being repeatedly targeted by a neighborhood bully, then parents need to get involved. Have a discussion with the bully's teachers or parents. But first, give your child a chance to defend themselves. Also, the last thing your children need is for you to start pointing an accusatory finger at them. They aren't the ones to blame and they weren't looking for trouble. Parents should never say things like, "I told you the kids would make fun of you if you started crying." Nor is it productive to make them feel deficient for not knowing how to defend themselves, or to compare them with another child who is better at it.

Laugh With Them, Not At Them

In order for your children to learn to take taunting lightly, without letting it hurt them, it's crucial that you set a good example. One mother, for instance, told her six-year-old daughter to make fun of her any time her hair got messed up. It became a game in which the girl would make up funny names for her mother. Then her mother would respond with a playful smile and say something funny to keep the joke going.

Laughing with your kids is fine, but laughing at them is a no-no. Language is a marvelous tool that should be used with great care. Sometimes a sarcastic comment slips out and you think it was inoffensive. But it wasn't. In fact, it may have been deeply hurtful. Always be careful what you say, and be ready to backpedal whenever your child's face says, "Enough!"

When children tell you that they are being made fun of, don't underestimate its importance. It's very serious and requires your attention—it may be a sign of low self-esteem or emotional immaturity. In any case, it can cause learning difficulties and problems in social interaction. If it becomes serious, and you've done all you can, psychotherapy can help your child overcome these issues and achieve a happy childhood and a successful future.

HOW TO RECOGNIZE ANXIETY

Everyone knows what anxiety feels like. Who hasn't had butterflies in their stomach before a first date with someone who's really attractive? Or what about the tension you feel when your boss goes on a rampage? Anxiety often forces you to act. For example, it can make you study harder for an exam or pay more attention to your personal appearance before a first date. Most of the time, anxiety is just a fleeting emotion. It can be normal or even a good thing. But when anxiety is a constant and affects many areas of your life, what you're facing is "Anxiety Disorder" (AD).

What is diagnosed as AD isn't just a problem of nerves, like when people say, "I'm nervous when I go on stage." It's an illness, and if left untreated, it can ruin your life and affect your relationships with the people you love.

It's common for several members of the same family to suffer from anxiety. You'll hear people say, "My sister's a nervous wreck, just like Mom." And it's something that is accepted as reality, something that can't be changed.

Anxiety is, however, an illness that can be cured with proper therapy.

Lisa, a young mother of two, says, "I always thought of myself as a fearful person, someone who can never manage to relax, even just in everyday situations. I'd become anxious trying to figure out what I was going to make for dinner, or what I was going to buy my best friend for her birthday. For days on end, I couldn't stop thinking about the same things over and over again, and I was so preoccupied about the little things that I couldn't even disconnect when I was making love to my husband. I'd have trouble sleeping, because my mind wouldn't let me stop thinking about what I had to do the next day. I couldn't even concentrate long enough to read the newspaper or watch a movie on TV. Sometimes my heart would start racing before friends came over to my house, and I'd get extremely worried if my daughter was ten minutes late from school."

AD is a lot more than just your normal, everyday anxiety. It's when just about anything triggers a feeling of fear and stress. It's when you're afraid before something happens, and you have this feeling that "something terrible is about to happen." Being excessively concerned about your health is also a form of anxiety. My stomach hurts. Could it be cancer?" So is an exaggerated fear of losing your money or being laid off. A persistent feeling that you're on the verge of disaster. Thoughts like these keep the sufferer in a constant state of stress.

People with AD are always worrying about something. If there's no reason to worry, they find one. They simply can't believe that peace and quiet or happiness can be a part of their lives. People with anxiety can't even relax when they're sleeping. Sometimes, they wake up in the middle of the night and can't get back to sleep.

Often, these fears are accompanied by physical

symptoms like trembling, muscle pain in the back and neck, headaches, irritability, shortness of breath, and sometimes, nausea or diarrhea. People with anxiety disorder get tired easily and experience long bouts of depression. Sometimes they feel like crying all the time without knowing why.

A lot of people begin having issues with anxiety when they are children or teenagers and that's why they say, "This is just the way I am." In reality, they just don't remember ever being any other way. But when these symptoms are more than just a way of being, psychotherapy is highly effective. People who get treated for anxiety usually start seeing results within a few months. Instead of being controlled by fear, anxiety and worry, they realize that they are the ones in control.

Panic Attacks

Many people who have AD also suffer from panic attacks. These attacks appear suddenly and without warning, and they are terrifying. People who suffer from panic attacks also get anxiety worrying about when their next attack will happen.

Common Symptoms of a Panic Attack:
- A racing heart
- Chest pain
- Dizziness
- Stomachaches or nausea
- Flushed cheeks
- Hot face
- Shortness of breath
- Terror
- A feeling of losing control
- Fear of dying
- Sweats

During panic attacks, some people feel like they're having a heart attack or that they are about to lose their mind, but these feelings usually only last a few minutes.

Recent studies indicate that about 6 million Americans have panic attacks, although this only takes into account reported cases, those who have sought help. Panic attacks are more common in women than in men.

Some victims of panic attacks try to avoid everyday situations that might trigger another attack, like driving a car or venturing out into the street alone. If they've had a panic attack in an elevator, they may develop a fear of elevators. And because they try to avoid situations that scare them, they often become dependent on other members of their family.

About a third of all panic attack sufferers develop a condition called Agoraphobia, the fear of open, crowded places. They don't go to family gatherings, and they avoid going out into the street or places like movie theaters. With proper psychotherapy, and in some cases, medication, studies show that people who suffer from panic attacks manage to overcome the problem within a relatively short period of time.

Phobias

A phobias is an irrational fear of a particular situation, object or animal.

Twenty-seven-year-old Martin tells us: "I feel like I'm going to die every time I board an airplane. When I take my seat and they close the doors, I feel trapped. My heart starts racing and I begin to sweat. I feel like I'm losing control. It's completely unbearable. It's not that I'm afraid of crashing, exactly, but I feel trapped. I'd rather not go on vacation at all than feel that way."

Many people are afraid of being on the top floor of a

skyscraper. Others are scared of stairs, tunnels, or being stuck in a traffic jam. Phobias are irrational. For instance, some people are afraid of going to the tenth floor of an office building, but have no problem skiing on tall mountains. Others may be scared to death of mice, but not tigers. People with phobias know that their fears are irrational, but they can't do anything about it. And being in a phobic situation can cause panic attacks.

These issues are often observed in several members of the same family and may begin in childhood or adolescence. However, phobias that emerge in adulthood tend to be much more persistent. It is estimated that 20 percent of all adults suffer from a phobia. And it can cause people to stop advancing in their personal lives or careers.

A lot of people don't get help for their phobia because they lack the information they need, and they end up dealing with these problems for years. However, most phobias can be resolved through psychotherapy and relaxation exercises—but first, the anxiety level has to be reduced.

When children suffer from anxiety, panic attacks and phobias, it is important to get them into treatment as soon as possible. These problems don't go away on their own. On the contrary, they get worse with time. Too many parents accept their children's anxiety as "natural," or they simply think "he's just like his father." But anxiety can cause problems at school. It is associated with symptoms like lack of concentration, nervousness, irritability, difficulty sleeping and so on. People with anxiety can't enjoy their lives, and it's a shame when a child can't enjoy their childhood because they suffer from an illness that is easily treatable.

EFFECTS OF AN ABSENTEE FATHER

How many times have you heard a woman complain about her husband, saying, "He won't face up to his problems. He doesn't make any decisions. I'm sick and tired of doing everything. All he does is go to work and come home and watch TV. I know he loves me, but I don't know what he'd do without me."

Amy has been married for four years, and she's ready to give up. She tells us she's decided to get a divorce. She didn't want to have children because she knew that the responsibility would fall on her. She's overwhelmed by her husband's behavior and his dependence on her. She says, "I don't know what he would do without me." And this is the key to the problem. On the one hand, Amy is proud to be needed. However, she feels like she's carrying a huge burden and she's exhausted. That's why she's decided to not have children and get a divorce.

If we look at the situation objectively, we see that Amy and her husband share the responsibility equally. Amy did all the work, and she always made the decisions. Her husband deferred to her more and more, until eventually, he gave up and stopped making any decisions at all. Amy slowly took control of nearly every aspect of their lives, and now her husband can no longer function without her. Amy's need to be in control, to be "indispensable," is rooted in her fear of abandonment.

When Amy was four years old, her father left home. Because she was an only child, all of her mother's attention was focused on her. She would see her mother cry, and hear her complain about "Men." "They're all alike. They build up your hopes, you get married, have kids, and then they go and leave without batting an eyelid." Amy's mother never married again and never got tired of generalizing that men were "all alike."

Meanwhile, Amy's suffering over not being able to see her father became intense. She got used to it, though, and started to feel like she no longer needed him. As a teenager, she was attracted to boys, but she was also shy and didn't open up easily. At a deeper level, and almost without being aware of it, she was afraid of falling in love. She didn't want to have to relive the intense pain of being abandoned by her father, which was consistently reinforced by her mother's words: "Men are all alike."

When Amy met her husband, she realized, subconsciously, that he was an emotionally dependent individual who was incapable of confronting situations himself. He gave her the feeling that "this is a man who will never leave me." Needy men don't leave, because they get used to having everything done for them. They depend on others, and that puts the woman in control. At the same time, though, behind every controlling woman is someone with a profound fear of being abandoned or cheated on. Over time, this situation cannot provide happiness for either person, and, sooner or later, the relationship ends, whether through his initiative or hers.

Amy perceived her mother's hatred for men, but she had also loved her father during the few years that they shared together. She started to feel that the only way to keep a man close was to be controlling and indispensable. In fact, Amy was so sure she would never be "abandoned" that she was the one who decided to "abandon" her husband by getting a divorce. A part of her already knew this would happen when she married a man like her husband.

How Can You Help Your Children

If you are someone who feels abandoned by your husband, try, first of all, to understand what is going on. Ask yourself how you got to this point. Don't blame yourself and try to be objective. It's important to process your feelings and not keep your anger and resentment bottled up. That will hurt both you and your children.

If you do manage to free yourself of your initial anger and understand what happened, try to avoid generalizing and blaming all men. This kind of message is damaging to children and can affect them for the rest of their lives. Boys will be affected in terms of their self-esteem, and girls in their relationships with men. Don't say negative things to them about their father because that only fills them with your own fury and rancor. These are *your* feelings, and they don't necessarily have to be your children's feelings, too. Talk to your children honestly about what happened, but don't fill them up with feelings that don't belong to them. And think about your how much you control them.

If you find that you have trouble facing these issues, seek professional help. Sometimes your emotions are so intense that you can't see clearly. And if that happens, you might say or do some things that have a profound effect on your children.

EMOTIONAL EFFECTS OF AN ABORTION

Nowadays, most women are aware that modern medicine has greatly reduced the physical risks of an abortion. But what many don't know is to what extent an abortion can affect them emotionally. Sometimes, women think that because they've stopped thinking about it, it won't affect their lives. But the truth is that the emotional effects of an abortion can last a lifetime. Although an abortion doesn't leave any physical scars, the emotional wound it causes can profoundly affect a woman's relationship with herself, her other children and her partner.

Some of the most common effects of having an abortion are:

Feeling Guilty
Some women feel guilty for not having allowed their child to live. In general, a woman thinks of her child—especially while it is living inside her—as an extension of

herself. She may feel that she has not allowed a part of her own self to live. Although she may have rationalized what led her to the decision, another part of her—the non-intellectual part—isn't satisfied by such explanations, and that makes her feel like a bad person. Later on, these feelings can subconsciously lead her to seek situations in which she will suffer, as a means of absolving herself of her guilt. Because many women feel like they "deserve" to suffer, they accept abusive relationships. After an abortion, it is also common for a woman to fear that she won't be able to get pregnant, that not being able to be a mother is their punishment for having an abortion. And this fear can be a psychological factor in preventing a new pregnancy.

A young mother tells us that she's worried because her four-year old is constantly saying "I can't" whenever he's presented with new situations. She always resolves his problems for him, and that's caused him to stop making any effort. "I solve every little problem for him," she tells us, "because I just want him to be happy. I don't want him to suffer. I want him to have it easy. But it seems like all I'm doing is making it so he doesn't want to do anything for himself. Now he wants everything done for him. I don't think he's ready for kindergarten yet. He acts like a child much younger than his age."

Clearly, this is a typical case of overprotection. With a little more questioning, we found out that the reason she wants to "do everything" for her son is that she is subconsciously trying to make up for her guilt over having an abortion when she was eighteen years old. She had practically forgotten about it. She said she never even thought about it. The abortion occurred before she was married. She was concerned about her family's reaction, and at the time, it wasn't possible to get married right away because of her boyfriend's financial status.

Meanwhile, her four-year-old son was being so overprotected—she was trying to give him everything that her aborted child would never be able to have—that she was actually damaging his self-esteem. When children have everything served up for them already resolved, and they're not given incentives to make an effort, they start to feel incapable of doing things on their own. The message is: "If they have to do everything for me, I must be *not be able* to do anything myself." When this message is etched into a child's subconscious, they won't feel like making an effort because they think it won't achieve anything. They'll want everything done for them, and they feel inferior. This makes children dependent, insecure, demanding and intolerant.

Depression and Suicidal Thoughts

Some women who have had an abortion experience depression. They lose the will to live and may lack energy. They may also feel like sleeping all the time, and are disconnected from other people. It is common for women to close themselves up in a dark room without wanting to see anyone. They may also become hypersensitive, crying for no apparent reason and being disproportionately affected by things. If these symptoms persist for more than two or three months, they can become chronic and require psychological treatment. In some cases, women with post-abortion symptoms may entertain thoughts of suicide, and if they are faced with emotionally difficult situations like being abandoned by a partner, marital infidelity, or the loss of a job—they may attempt it. If this is the case, seek therapy with a skilled professional.

Emotional Disconnection from other Children

Women who have had an abortion may withdraw into themselves, feeling guilty and emotionally disconnected

PARENTING TODAY

from their other children. That can have serious consequences for their children, because they may feel unloved by their mother. In cases like these, they may start doing things to draw attention to themselves. They may become restless or disobedient to get back their mother, who seems to be "in her own world" and doesn't give them the attention they need.

Effects on Sexuality

Women who have had an abortion may feel an excessive fear of a new pregnancy. This can cause a lot of anxiety, especially during sexual intercourse. They may not be fully present during sex, or even avoid it altogether. At some level, they may also blame their husband for the decision to have an abortion, maybe because it was his suggestion or he pressured her to have it. Or maybe he insists on having sex, or didn't use protection.

If a woman is angry or hurt, it will be hard for her to have harmonious sexual relations. Women's sexuality is connected to their emotional state, and when they feel resentment, rage or pain, they just can't get in the mood. That can leave both partners unsatisfied, and it may lead to infidelity.

Eating Disorders

After an abortion, women frequently demonstrate changes in their eating patterns—they may start overeating, especially sweets. They may seek pleasure in food to compensate for their pain and guilt—or they might "punish" themselves by not eating. Either way, the consequences can be serious.

149

WHEN PARENTS ARGUE

When children come to therapy, a lot of parents act as if they were leaving us a broken radio, and they expect us to return it to them in good working order. But often when a therapist starts working with a child, they find out that a big part of the problem originates in the family environment, and more specifically, in the parents' relationship with one another.

Maria has two boys, age two and four. She has brought her older son, Jack, to therapy. Maria tells us that Jack is disobedient, and she has to yell and repeat things ten times until he gets it. He yells back at her, "You don't know anything! Shut up and leave me alone!" And on top of that, he threatens, "When Daddy gets home, I'm gonna tell him you hit me!"

Maria continues, "The worst thing of all is that when my husband gets home, Jack tells him his side of the story, and it always ends up making me look bad. My husband gets mad at me and says I have no patience, that I punish him too much. And sometimes he threatens me, and says he's going to take the boys to my mother-in-law's house so she can raise them." Maria says, "If I punish my son for not finishing his chores, his father just lets him off when he gets home." The result: "I'm powerless. My son doesn't listen to me and there's nothing I can do about it. The situation is unbearable. I'm a nervous wreck, and everything seems to get under my skin. As a mother, I sometimes feel frustrated. My kids don't listen to me, they don't respect me, and the only thing my husband does is criticize and threaten me. I feel like Jack doesn't love me as a mother. He'll only obey his father. And worse still, my youngest is following in his big brother's footsteps."

When we told Maria that the problem wasn't Jack, and that she and her husband needed therapy, she looked surprised and said, "But if Jack would just listen to me, there wouldn't be a problem."

A lot of parents have trouble accepting the fact that their children's issues are very often less important than the relationship between their parents. Jack Sr. undermines Maria's authority, showing his two boys that everything their mother says is wrong. And to drive the point home even further, Maria's husband says—in front of the children—that his sons would be better off with his mother. The message that Jack and his little brother get from their father is, "Don't listen to your mother. What she says doesn't count, and if she hits you, I want to know about it. What I say is the only thing that matters around here." This message doesn't even have to be expressed in words—it can be conveyed through actions.

Since Jack and his little brother are boys, they need to identify with their father. Boys start forming their sexual identity between the age of three and five. They emulate their father, who they consider a hero, someone who never makes a mistake. If the boys see their hero treating their mother with contempt, humiliating her and undermining her authority, they begin to think that they should do the same thing. And so a pattern is formed in which the woman's word doesn't matter.

The problem here is rooted in the relationship between Maria and Jack Sr., who don't communicate well or have a relationship based on respect. If Maria takes away Jack's TV privileges for not doing what he has been told to do, Jack Sr. needs to support her decision. Parents need a united front to prevent their children from taking advantage of them. Little Jack manipulates his mother by saying, "I'm telling Daddy on you when he gets home." He knows that this will make his mother think twice, and if it's worked before, he'll continue using this tactic—unless his father makes a change. Jack and Maria need to agree on how to set limits for their children and how to discipline them.

When communication breaks down and parents can't agree, it's because they both want to be "right" or because they don't listen to one another. If they can't agree on how to deal with their children, then they probably won't be able to agree on anything else, either. The problem begins with the couple. The attitude of the children is just the result of the lack of communication and mutual respect between Maria and Jack.

But the father is not the only one responsible for the situation. The mother doesn't demand respect, and she allows herself to be belittled because she is insecure and has low self-esteem. She suffers and complains, but she doesn't do anything about it. Jack and Maria need couple's therapy so they can learn how to communicate, to respect one another and to listen. Maria's children will regain their respect for her and learn to obey only when the issues between husband and wife are resolved.

If a child picks fights and becomes aggressive, it's

probably because they've seen their parents fighting. If children see that their parents don't listen to one another, they won't learn to listen either. If children see their parents disrespecting each other, they will learn to treat others with disrespect, too.

You can prevent years of pain and suffering, and even a divorce, with couple's therapy. Above all, you'll avoid the negative consequences to your children.

If you have a toothache, you go to the dentist, so why not go to a psychologist when your soul is in pain? The soul is in the realm of emotion, and it's what we psychologists are trained to work with. It doesn't mean you're crazy if you see a psychologist. Psychologists serve people who want to improve their lives, resolve their issues and live in harmony with their loved ones.

The experience of therapy is one of learning and growth. It helps you figure out how to solve your problems, how to face life, and fight your jealousy, insecurity, and fear. If you have issues with your partner, don't wait until it's too late, when your children start feeling the consequences. You deserve to live life fully and be happy, and if you always blame other people when things go wrong, you'll never do what you need to do to change yourself.

DRUGS AND ALCOHOL

A lot of parents think the task of keeping their kids away from drugs and alcohol begins during adolescence, when their children turn 12 or 13, but in reality, the prevention process begins when your child is an infant.

Many parents also believe that some friends are a "bad influence" and they are the ones that cause children to drink or use drugs. However, the consumption of addictive substances begins when both "environmental" and "triggering" factors are involved.

Bad influences are just a "triggering" factor, but unless the child has the prerequisite environmental conditions, they will still say no when they are pressured to use. These environmental conditions make all the difference.

Environmental Conditions
Escape
These are the mechanisms that a child first learns as an infant. For example, let's say a child gets scared or their stomach hurts, and they start crying. If their mother gives

them a pacifier dipped in sugar, the baby immediately tastes the sweetness and stops crying. But when the sugar is gone, they begin crying again, and their mother gives them some more.

Rather than confronting the issue, what the child learns is that when they get scared or if something hurts, the feeling gets covered up by something pleasurable (sugar). In the future, the pleasurable thing could be something sweet, or it could be a cigarette, alcohol or drugs.

On the other hand, if the child's mother gets close and tries to figure out why baby is crying, if she looks to see if the diaper is wet and uses her mother's intuition to figure out if something is hurting or if something scared the baby, if she takes her baby in her arms to soothe her child, then they will learn to confront their problems, rather than escape.

Children learn escape mechanisms early on. And later, the perfect escape mechanism becomes alcohol and especially marijuana, which creates a state of calm and contentedness that a young person doesn't have in their real life.

Overprotection

If you overprotect your child and don't encourage them to develop their skills, they will grow up fearful, insecure and they'll seek the support of other people or things. They'll feel like they can't do it on their own.

If everything is resolved for them early on, then by the time they reach adolescence and are forced to start resolving their own issues, they will seek the support of things that give them a sense of security, like a cigarette between their fingers, or a sip of alcohol that makes them feel like Superman, not to mention stimulants like cocaine that create a sense of invincibility.

Low self-esteem

Low self-esteem creates a feeling of worthlessness. Children with low self-esteem don't love themselves. They think they are not important and they "can't." After those first few sips of beer, when they find out that they are able to do all the things they thought they couldn't do, they'll want to have more—and that's how addiction begins.

When a 14-year old child doesn't feel brave enough to kiss a girl they like, and they realize that after a few sips of alcohol they not only find the courage to kiss the girl, but also to tell them they like them, they'll want to do it again. Alcohol brings out personality traits they never thought they had.

Many young people tell me they began drinking and smoking marijuana to be close to the popular kids at school. This occurs when a young person doesn't have a sense of self-worth, and they feel they can only get that self-worth when they are close to other people who are respected and popular.

Low self-esteem causes kids to want to excel through negative actions, not positive ones.

Depression or Anxiety

Young children who have depression or anxiety are at risk for drugs and/or alcohol when they become teenagers. Young people who are depressed lack motivation and energy. They don't have a sense of purpose and they're sad and oversensitive.

Stimulants like crack or cocaine give them energy, motivation, and a good mood, while numbing their pain.

In the case of anxiety, something similar happens— cigarettes, alcohol and marijuana calm their nerves. They create a sense of relaxation that a young person doesn't get any other way.

The main reasons why kids start using drugs and alcohol is to calm down, escape from their problems, and to feel better generally.

Social Factors

Our society encourages young men to drink so they can "be a man." Young people believe that they can't have fun without alcohol. These are beliefs that young people pick up from the world around them.

Parents who Drink

When a child grows up seeing one of their parents drinking, they think it's normal, and they also think that they have to do it to be an adult. Parents don't have the authority to tell their kids that drinking is bad for your heath if they don't set a good example themselves.

Adolescence is a time of huge physical and emotional changes. Young people are faced with a lot of new things, and they start to test themselves and compare themselves to other people. They begin to look for belonging in a group. If they get to this stage of life with low self-esteem, insecurity, depression or anxiety, they are much more at risk than young people who are secure with themselves and stable emotionally.

When there is a lot of fighting at home, a hostile environment or too much criticism, a young person will try to "escape," and the perfect way to do that is through drugs.

Some Common Signs of Drug or Alcohol Abuse in Teenagers:

- A racing heart
- Chest pains
- Dizziness

- Physical signs: fatigue; difficulty sleeping; repeated health complaints; dull, red eyes; a persistent cough.
- Emotional signs: changes in personality, mood swings, irritability, not taking care of their responsibilities, low self-esteem, bad judgment, depression, withdrawal and lack of interest.
- At home: starting arguments, disobeying rules, avoidance and lack of communication with other family members.
- At school: lack of interest, a negative attitude, bad grades, frequent absences, not completing their assignments and disciplinary issues.
- In their community: having friends that are involved with drugs and alcohol, problems with the law, and a drastic change in their clothing or appearance in general.

Some of these warning signs can also indicate other emotional problems. If you suspect the use or abuse of drugs and alcohol, a trained mental health professional can do a comprehensive evaluation.

Parents can help their children by educating them about drugs and alcohol at an early age, establishing open communication, being good role models, and watching out for and dealing with problems as they arise.

If you suspect that your child is using drugs:

- Don't overreact with insults, threats or shouting.
- Resist the urge to go through your child's room in search of evidence.
- Express your concern at a time when both of you are calm.
- If your child is using drugs, don't issue ultimatums.
- If your child is in trouble with the police or has to go to court, support them and help them get through the consequences, but don't try to avoid them.

- Inform them about the effects of the drugs they are using.
- Try to figure out how long they have been using the drug, or if it was their first time.
- Seek professional help.

If you suspect that your child is using drugs, but you don't have any proof, take them to a doctor and ask for a drug test.

Some Statistics

- Young people whose parents talk to them regularly about the dangers of drugs have a 42% lower chance of using them compared to parents who don't discuss it. Only one out of four young people report having had that conversation.[1]
- Alcohol is the most commonly used drug among teenagers.[2]
- Teenagers who use alcohol have a 50% higher chance of using cocaine than teens who don't drink.[2]
- 40% of young people who start drinking alcohol before the age of14 develop alcoholism, compared to 10% who start after the age of 20.[2]
- 65% of young people who drink report having been given alcohol by friends or relatives.[2]
- 28% of teenagers have a friend or acquaintance who has used ecstasy, and 17% know more than two people who have used it.[3]
- By the eighth grade, 52% of adolescents have tried alcohol, 41% have used cigarettes, and 20% have used marijuana.[2]
- In 2000, over 60% of teenagers said that drugs were used or sold in their schools.[3]

[1] Partnership for a Drug-Free America
[2] Substance Abuse: *The Nation's Number One Health Problem*
[3] U.S. Department of Health & Human Services

RISKS OF THE INTERNET

Everyone knows that the internet is convenient and it gives us a lot of options, but it is also important to keep in mind the risks for young children and teenagers.

A lot of parents think that because their child is locked in their room sitting in front of a computer screen that there are no dangers involved. But with just a single click, a young person can access sites that promote the sale and abuse of drugs, manuals to create homemade bombs, clear instructions on how to kill a person without leaving any evidence, and the most extensive collection of pornography in the world.

Internet use becomes a problem when the number of hours your child spends at the computer begins to affect the normal development of their daily lives, or when it changes their mood, or affects their studies.

If parents don't set limits, their children may access websites that are inappropriate for their age.

Risks Associated with the Internet

- Difficulty focusing or spending an excessive amount of time looking things up.
- Accessing unreliable or false information.
- Accessing sexual, pornographic or violent websites.
- Pages that promote drugs and alcohol, or prescription pills.
- Sites that advocate racist or sexist ideologies, or dangerous sects or groups.
- Access to black market websites.
- Contact with people who have created a false identity to lure people into sexual, violent or criminal acts.
- Children can receive threats or find themselves in situations in which they are abused or harassed.
- Teenagers may be tempted to purchase things without their parents' permission.
- Credit card numbers may be used fraudulently by others or stolen.

Your child may be addicted to the internet if they can't control the amount of time they spend surfing the net, or if they neglect their other responsibilities, their sleep, or their hygiene. Other signs of internet addiction include neglecting their friends and acquaintances, avoiding physical activities or getting irritated when they are asked to get off the computer.

What should parents do?

- Set limits on the amount of time your children spend on the internet—it should be no more than one hour per day.
- Show your children where to find good sources of information.

- It may be a good idea to use a timer to indicate when the computer should be turned off.
- Help your children develop critical thinking skills.
- Let them know about the danger of giving out personal information through the internet.
- Install internet safety programs that can limit their access to certain pages.
- Warn them about the dangers of contacting strangers.

Social networking sites are especially risky when they are used by children with low self-esteem, or those whose social skills are not as developed.

Children can feel lonely even if they have hundreds of friends on these sites, and lack of real communication with their parents can lead to severe depression.

They can also be humiliated or shamed, and that could even lead to suicide.

Chat

Another big risk is the chat—online communication with friends, acquaintances, family members, or someone else from anywhere in the world.

Online chat exposes young people to strangers whose influence could be harmful to them. It can encourage virtual relationships which lack commitment and don't involve feelings—and that could result in insecurity or anxiety. Instead of having to resolve conflicts, these relationships can often just be ended with a click. This doesn't benefit young peoples' social skills or their ability to handle their emotions. Because these sites are anonymous, they attract people who are introverted, shy, antisocial, sexually perverted, psychopathic, as well as people who are rapists, scammers, or just mentally ill. And a person can use fake names and pictures to draw in young people and get information from them.

Some suggestions on chatting

1. Encourage your children to use private chat rooms so they can choose their contacts and communicate with people they know.
2. Insist that your children don't give out any personal information or communicate with strangers.
3. Try to prevent them from meeting with people they don't know.

Sexting

This word is a combination of "sex" and "text," and is used to designate the exchange of sexually-explicit photographs through the internet. Nowadays, teenagers use their cell phones to send and receive these photos. It has become common, yet most young people don't understand the legal and emotional consequences of it.

It is important for parents to discuss this issue with their children before handing them a cell phone.

When a minor sends a "sext" of themselves, it can be considered child pornography, and that can cause legal problems for parents and their children.

A lot of problems can be avoided when you make time to talk to your children, and above all, to listen to them. When technology becomes the babysitter, the whole family pays the consequences. And usually, quality is more important than quantity when it comes to spending time with your children.

My intention with this book is to help parents who are raising children in today's world, in which things are changing so fast that everything is new, and there are no models to follow. Parents have to make their own individual path—because every child and every parent is special and unique.

6307036R00103

Printed in Great Britain
by Amazon.co.uk, Ltd.,
Marston Gate.